Opie Percival Read

Bolanyo

A Novel

Opie Percival Read

Bolanyo
A Novel

ISBN/EAN: 9783337042042

Printed in Europe, USA, Canada, Australia, Japan

Cover: Foto ©ninafisch / pixelio.de

More available books at **www.hansebooks.com**

BOLANYO
A NOVEL
by
OPIE READ
author of
A Kentucky Colonel
The Jucklins
etc

CHICAGO
Printed for
Way & Williams

MDCCCXCVII

CONTENTS.

BOLANYO

CHAPTER I.

ON THE RIVER.

ON the night of the 26th of April our company closed an engagement at the St. Charles Theater in New Orleans; and before the clocks began to strike the hour of twelve, our bags and baggage had been tumbled on board a steamboat headed for St. Louis. The prospects of the National Dramatic

Company had been bright; competent critics had pronounced our new play a work of true and sympathetic art, before production, but had slashed at our tender vitals when the piece had passed from rehearsal to presentation.   The bad beginning in the East had not truthfully foretold a good ending in the South.   The people had failed to sympathize with our "Work of Sympathetic Art."   Hope had leaped from town to town; was always sure to fall, but always quick to rise again; and, now, three nights in St. Louis would close the season, and doubtless end the career of the National Dramatic Company.   The captain of the Red Fox, a dingy, waterlogged and laborious craft, had kindly offered to let us come aboard at half his usual rate.   He assured our manager that this concession afforded a real pleasure; that he held a keen interest in our profession, having years ago done a clog dance as a negro minstrel.   Necessity oozed oil upon this unconscious sarcasm, and with grateful dignity the captain's offer was accepted.

By two o'clock we were creaking and churning against the current, and, alone in a begrimed cubby-hole, with a looking-glass shaking against the frail wall, I lay down with a sigh to take stock of myself. Hope had been agile, but now it did not bound with so light a spring. Could it be that I had begun to question my ability as an actor? It was true that the critics had slit me with their knives, but the people had frequently applauded, and, after all, the people deliver the verdict. The judge may charge, but the jury pronounces. I knew then, as I know now, that there must be a reserve force behind all forms of art; that one essential of artistic expression is to create the belief that you are not doing your best, that you are not under a strain. And I thought that I had accomplished this, but the critics had said that my restraint was weak and my passion overwrought. I had not come out as a star. As a stock comedian I had been granted a kindly mention, and had accepted the place of leading man,

but this had given offense and had called
forth an unjust tirade of censure.   Perhaps
I had assumed a little too much, but the
man who is not ready to assume will never
accomplish anything, and from a lower station must be content to contemplate the
success of those who were less delicate.

When morning came I looked out upon
the canefields, green to the edge of the
horizon.   The breakfast bell rang, but I
hung back, not for lack of appetite, but for
the reason that the other members of the
company had ceased to be companiona-
ble.   Even a meager applause can excite,
if not envy, a certain degree of contempt;
and the small stint of approbation which,
like a mere crumb, had fallen to me could
not have aroused the jealousy, but surely
sharpened the sarcasms, of my fellow-players.   In a side remark intended for me, and
which struck me like a shaft, Culpepper, as
vain a fellow as ever mismumbled an author's lines, remarked to Miss Hatch that
an elephant would stretch his chain to reach

a bonbon. And, stroking as brutish a pug as ever found soft luxury in a woman's lap, she replied that it was a pity that the average theatrical elephant, foisted upon an easy manager, could only rival the real beast in clumsiness and in his appetite for sweets. So I waited, gazing out upon the edgeless spread of cane-land, until my companions in "sympathetic art" had indulged in the usual growl over their morning meal, and then I went out to breakfast. At the table sat one person, an oldish man with a dash of red in his countenance. As I sat down he looked up, and, with a pleasing smile, inquired if I were Mr. Maurice Belford. And when I had told him yes, he said:

"I thought so, or 'mistrusted' as much, as Old Bill Brooks used to say," he added, laughing. "Didn't know old Bill, I take it? Used to travel a good deal up and down the river, and was a great hand to go to a show. And he'd always set 'em through. No, sir, he wouldn't leave you. And this puts me in mind that I saw you play the other night. You caught me, I tell you. That character of *Tobe Wilson*, the gambler, was about as true a thing as I ever saw."

"I am much pleased to hear you say so," I replied, warming toward him. "But the critics said it was overdone and unreal," I added.

"The critics said so; who are they?"

"The newspaper representatives who come to the theater to find fault," I answered.

"Oh, that's it, eh? I didn't see what any of 'em said, and it wouldn't make any difference if I had. I've been a pilot on this river mighty nigh ever since I was a boy, and if I don't know what a real gambler is, I'd like for some man to point one out to me."

"I am really delighted to meet you, for surely your opinion is worth a great deal."

"Don't know about that," he replied, "but I know what a gambler is. Why, I set all the way through your show. Fellow wanted me to go out with him, but I wouldn't. And right by me set Senator Giles Talcom, of Mississippi. I live in Bolanyo, his town. It's improved mightily in the last twenty-five years. Got a new city hall, and some Dutchmen from the north are talking about starting a brewery. Now, Talcom is a smart man and he liked your show; said he was sorry you are to skip Bolanyo on your way up the river. As soon as I git a bite to eat I'm going up to take the wheel. Wouldn't you like to sit in the pilot house?''

Glad to accept the invitation of one who had the insight to recognize an artistic delineation of character, and the graciousness to declare it, I went with him to the pilot house. He took the wheel from a man who, I thought, did not look upon me kindly, and continued to talk, while with an intentness that traced a frown upon his brow he estimated the strength of the current, or the depth of the water on a shoal.

The river was low; the winter had been comparatively dry; the early spring thaw had spent its force, and there was as yet no premonitory swell of the great summer rise. The morning was sunless and soft, and far away a dragon-shaped mist lay low upon the land, a giant's nightmare, fading in the pale light of a reluctant day.

"The old river's dead," said the pilot, with the reverberations of a knell in the tone of his voice. "Look at that thing fluttering along over there, where the Lee and the Natchez used to plow. No, sir, the old Mississippi ain't much better than a sewer now. But she was a roarer back yonder in my time, I tell you. Ah, Lord, some great men have piloted palaces along here."

"Whom do you regard as the greatest?" I inquired, expecting to hear him pronounce a name well known to the stage and to literature.

"Well, of course there's a difference of opinion among them that don't know, but with them that do know there never was a pilot that could hold a candle to old Lige Patton."

"I don't believe I ever heard of him," I replied.

"Hah!" He turned his eyes upon me, with the up-river search still strong in his gaze, but as with a snatch he jerked them away and threw them upon a split in the current far ahead. "That might be," he assented, slowly turning his wheel. "I can jump off here most anywhere and find you a man that never heard of Julius Cæsar."

I preferred to remain silent under this rebuke, and he did not speak again until we had sheered off to the left of the split in the current, a snag, and then he said:

"Lige didn't weigh more than a hundred and sixty pounds at his best, and the boys used to say there wan't no meat on him at all, nothing but nerve. Game!" He cleared his throat, gave me a mere glance and continued: "It was said that a panther once met him in the woods, and gave vent to a most unearthly squall, which meant, 'excuse me, Mr. Patton,' and took to his heels and never was heard of in that section after that—the panther wan't—although he had been mighty popular among the pigs and sheep of that neighborhood. But Lige never killed many men. Never killed except when he was overpersuaded. · Gave up a good position once and went all the way to Jackson to call the governor of Mississippi a liar. And what was that for? Why, the governor issued a thanksgiving proclamation in spite of the fact that the river had been low for three months, making it pretty tough work for the pilots; and Lige, he declared that a governor who said that the people ought to be thankful was a liar. And I've got a little more religion now than I had at that time, but blamed if I don't still think he was right. I spoke a while ago of Senator Talcom, who lives in my town. Well, sir, Lige give Talcom his start in the world. It was this way: Lige wan't altogether a lamb when he was drinking; he sorter looked for a fight, but, understand, he didn't want to kill anybody, unless *over*persuaded. Talcom was a young fellow, at that time, and had just come to town. And, somehow, he got in Lige's way, and they fought. And if there ever was a man that had more wire than Lige, it was Talcom. It must have been some sort of an accident, but, somehow, he got the upper hand of Lige, got him down, got out his knife, and was about to cut his throat, when Lige said: 'Young fellow, you may put out my light as soon as you please, for you can do it, but there's one thing, and one thing only, that I'd like to live for, and that is to see what you are going to make of yourself.' Blamed if this didn't tickle Talcom, and he got up and flung his knife away. And, now to the point, sir; Lige went all around and told it that Talcom whipped him, and that was the making of Talcom. Now look at him —been in the State Senate year after year. Yes, sir," he added, "I reckon that in one

way and another Lige Patton developed
more men than anybody that ever struck
this country."

CHAPTER II.

IN THE AIR.

A T the noon hour my friend was re-
lieved, and together we went down
to dinner. Miss Hatch and Culpepper fell to whispering as soon
as I sat down, opposite them. I knew that
I was under a spiteful discussion, but, with
the appearance of paying no heed to them,
I remarked to the pilot, who sat beside me:

"You have often noticed, I suppose, that
human nature by turns partakes of the nature of all other animals, particularly of the
black cat and the yellow dog?"

"I don't know that I get you, exactly,
but go ahead," he replied.

This afforded Miss Hatch and Culpepper
an opportunity to titter. I did not look at
them, but addressed myself to the pilot.

"I confess that my meaning might have been clearer, but behind it lies a sufficient cause for its utterance."

He put down his knife and looked at me helplessly, shook his head as if puzzled, and fell to eating with this not very comforting observation:

"Jerk me out of bed any time of night, along here, and I can tell you where I am, and I am pretty good at foreseeing a change in the channel, but once in a while I strike a thing that I can't figger out, and I reckon you've just handed me one."

Miss Hatch was now so occupied with feeding her dog that she had no time to titter at my discomfiture, but I caught sight of Culpepper's hateful and invidious smile.

The meal was finished in silence, and I thought that the pilot had forgotten my clouded remark, but when he had resumed his place at the wheel, he cut his sharp old eye at me and said:

"But there are a good many things I can see, and one of them is, that you and them other show folks don't get along together very well."

"It's their fault," I replied.

"Of course," he rejoined, giving me a mere glimpse of his old eye, and this time it was not merely shrewd—it was rascally.

"I have done my best to merit their friendship," I said, somewhat sharply. "But they spurn me, they insinuate that I am an elephant on the manager's hands, when you yourself have been kind enough to tell me that my part of the performance was—"

"Good, first-rate," he broke in. "But in the play you almost have a set of love jimjams on account of that woman, and let her reform you, and all that sort of thing. It beats me," he added, shaking his head. "I don't see how a man can love and cavort with a woman one minute, and hate her the next. I pass, when it comes to that."

"The stage is a strange world," I replied.

"Yes, seems so. Hard way to earn money, hugging someone you don't like. Why, I know a woman I wouldn't hug for a thousand dollars. You appear to be a man of fair average sense. Why don't you go into some other business—why don't you go to work?"

"Work!" I cried, and I laughed so loud that a half naked boy on the shore tossed up his hat and shouted a salute to my merriment.

With his face hard set, and with his eyes sweeping the river, he waited for my attention, and then he said: "Yes, work. Of course it's all right for idle and shiftless fellows to go around this way, but it strikes me—of course I don't know—but it strikes me that if you were to get down to it, you might make something of yourself. It would be all right if you could make a great actor out of yourself, for then it would be worth your while, but always to be an under dog in the fight—"

"You are not a flatterer," I broke in.

"Well, I don't flatter men very much. Flattery, like feathers and ribbons, was intended for women; but even they are getting too much sense to swallow it. Come to think about it, they don't look for it as much as men do."

We had turned a bend, and the pilot, pointing, directed my eye toward a town. "There's old Bolanyo," he said. "One of the best towns on the river, one way and another. I live there when I'm at home. And that's where Senator Talcom lives, and that's where he had his fight with Lige Patton. I'm going to hop off there to see my folks. House so plain up there is the new city hall—must have cost forty-five thousand. Can't see Talcom's house; it's off in the far edge of the town. It's almost a farm, and I reckon he's got the finest magnolia garden in this whole section. Old Bowie, father of the Bowie knife, fought a duel right over yonder. Got his man. Stevens is coming up to relieve me now in a minute. Coming now, I believe. Just

2

step outside," he added, as his assistant appeared at the door, "and I'll show you the places of interest, and then trot down in time to hop off."

We stood near the pilot house, and, continuing to talk, he pointed out, with the finger of local pride, a number of buildings which he believed would be of interest to me, but his words fell without meaning. A lulling essence was exhaled by the town. A spirit of rest and contentment lay upon her lazy wharf. I heard the languid song of the indolent "white trash," and the happy-go-lucky haw-haw of the trifling negro. Through the lattice of a thin cloud the sun shot a glance, and the gilded plow on the courthouse dome stood at the end of a furrow of fire.

"Well, got to leave you."

He seized my hand, and at that moment I thought that I was jerked off my feet, high in the air, and then came a thunder clap so loud, so deafening that my senses were killed, conscious only that my body was a dead weight and that my mind had been shattered and blown away. It seemed that I was propelled through a long and vague interval of time, and then a plunge and a chill, and my senses fluttered with painful life. The sharp knowledge of an awful calamity shot through me—the boat had exploded her boilers and I had been blown into the river.

CHAPTER III.

THE BLACK GIANT.

I REMEMBER to have struggled, and to have been tumbled over and over by the current. I might have caught at a straw, but no array of sins came up for review, though there were enough of them scattered between my cradle bed and the bed of this engulfing river. But I thought of many a foolish thing, a pair of red-top boots, a whistle made of willow, a 'coon skin tacked against the wall of a negro's cabin; but I do not remember being taken out of the water, so I must have endured all the popular agonies of drowning. I have a faint recollection of being borne along at full length, of seeing lights and of hearing voices. Sometimes the voices were close and loud in my ears, and again they

were far away. Struggling reason sank
once more, an obliterating darkness fell;
and when, after a long time, the light returned, I realized that I was in a room,
lying on a bed. My nostrils were filled
with the pungent scent of liniments. A
tight bandage was about my head; and a
heavy sense of soreness told me that my
right side was crushed. I thought to say
something, but the pungent odor grew
stronger in my nostrils, and I sank to sleep.
When I awoke again the day was broad.
And never before had I realized what broad
day meant; it was the opposite of the sharp
and narrow lights that had shot out of
the thick darkness enshrouding my mind.
Everything was clear to me now. The explosion had occurred at the moment when
the pilot took my hand. But was I now
on board another steamer? No, my apartment was too spacious and too stately.
There were pictures on the walls, and on the
mantel stood a marble statuette—the Diver.
Undoubtedly I had been brought into a pri-

vate house, for no hospital would offer such luxury to a stranger. I heard footsteps and voices. The door was carefully opened and two men entered the room. Upon seeing my eyes turned toward them they advanced cheerfully. I tried to say good morning, but the words stuck in my throat. One of the men placed his fingers on my wrist and asked me how I felt. This time my effort at speech was more of a success, and I managed to tell him that I was beginning to feel very well, that I was thankful for the light, and that I hoped he would not administer any more of that stifling liniment.

"The ether," he said, speaking to his companion; and then to me he added, "No, you won't need any more of that. Well," he continued, turning again to his companion, "he's doing first rate. I'll be around again about eleven o'clock."

A sudden alarm came upon me. "Let me ask you a question," I cried as he turned to leave. "Haven't you cut off one of my legs?"

"No, sir-ree," he good-humoredly laughed.

"But I want you to be sure about it," I persisted. "Just this minute I tried to find them both but couldn't."

"Here, doctor," said the other man, "show, him that his legs are all right. Don't leave him in this fix."

"Yes, of course," said the doctor, and lifting the cover he proved that I had not been robbed by the surgeon's knife. "Got both arms, too, you see."

"But I'm pretty badly hurt."

"Well, the blow-up didn't do you any particular good, but you are coming along all right. All we've got to guard against now is a rise in temperature, and there'll be no danger of that if you keep quiet."

"But the other members of the company. Tell me about them."

"They're all right—the most of them. You shall have all the details in due time, but now you must keep quiet."

They went out, closing the door softly, and I dozed off to sleep; and when I awoke

I was thankful to find that the day was still broad. I was conscious that someone was in the room, and, slightly turning, I beheld an enormous negro, standing in the middle of the floor, looking at me.

"You have had a good sleep, Sir," he said, "and I have waited for you to awake so that I could give you some refreshment."

He spoke with a precision that was almost painful, as if he were translating a sentence from a dead language, and my look must have betrayed my astonishment, for his thick lips parted in a smile, broad, but sedate. He appeared to be pleased at my surprise, and, smiling again, he bowed and quitted the room, but soon returned with a tray which he placed on a chair near the bed.

"Here is something which the physician has pronounced good for you to eat," he said, "but don't try to sit up. Here, let me get my arm under you, this way. Now we have it."

"Take it away, I'm not hungry," I said,

after finding the position too painful to endure. He eased me down, put the chair back and stood looking at me.

"Won't you sit down?"

"No, I thank you, Sir."

"But it makes me tired to see you stand."

"Then, Sir, I will sit down." He brought another chair, and, seating himself, he turned his searching eyes upon me. He was so enormous and he towered so, even after sitting down, that he inspired a feeling of creepy dread, his eyes so black and his smile so grave; and I was sure that in his presence the day could not long continue to be broad; indeed, I could see that the light at the window was slowly fading.

"I asked them if I might come and nurse you," he said. "There were other stricken ones that I might have nursed, but I heard that you were an actor, and then I knew where my duty lay."

"I am thankful for your partiality to my profession, at any rate," I replied.

He smiled, and his great teeth gleamed in the fading light. "I was not influenced by the partiality of the flesh, but by the duty laid upon the spirit. Most anyone could nurse your body, but I begged the privilege of nursing your soul as well."

"Ah, and you think an actor's soul is in especial need of nursing?"

"With your permission we will leave that for some future converse. I have been enjoined not to engage you in a talk that might bring weariness upon you. For a few nights to come there may be danger, and until that time is—is—shall have been passed, I will sit with you."

"But who are you?" I inquired.

"I am the humblest servant of the church wherein I preach the gospel that sinners may be brought to repentance; and my name is Washington Smith. But I must talk no more, and you must keep quiet."

"But where am I? Tell me that."

"You are in good hands, and the Lord and his servants are watching over you.

But I must request you not to speak again to-night."

He took up the tray and went out, and when he returned he sat down, though not upon a chair, but upon the floor, with his back against the wall.

CHAPTER IV.

THE SENATOR.

WHENEVER I awoke in the course of that long and dreary night, it was to find the black giant standing near the bedside. Once his hand, like the wing of a buzzard, passed over me, and I muttered a complaint. "I just wanted to determine whether or not you had a fever, Sir," he said. "You were talking in your sleep, and I thought it best to investigate the state of your temperature. But you are all right."

I was half asleep and doubtless could not at morning have remembered a strain of music or a bit of pleasantry, but at daylight his stilted words were clear in my mind. I looked about for him but he was gone. Breakfast was brought in by a negress, tall enough to be his wife. I asked her if she were, and, showing me her teeth, she assured me that she was an old maid; that no man, even if one of the best preachers in the Lord's church, should be her master. She said that she had married one man on trial, but that, after living with her a year or more, he had robbed her of a silver piece and run away; and now she was going to teach her daughter never to take a man except on suspicion, and to be mighty careful even then. The amusement that she offered assisted me to eat. She talked incessantly during the time, and as she took up the tray to go out, the doctor and the gentleman who had advised him to prove to me that I was still possessed of both legs came into the room.

"Oh, he's all right," said the woman. "Yas, sah, an' you got ter take 'em wid 'spicion even if da is hurt."

The doctor pronounced me much improved, cut short his visit, and left me with his friend, at whom I now looked with considerable interest. He was of a manly build, dressed in a black "Prince Albert" coat, buttoned below, but opened out wide at the breast. The ends of his grayish mustache were slightly twisted, and on his chin was a "dab" of whiskers. He appeared to be proud of his bearing, and proud of the belief that no one could discover the seat of his pride. He moved about rather gracefully, carrying a soft hat in his hand, as if he were ready to salute a gentleman or bow profoundly to a lady.

"Pardon me, Sir," I began, and he turned toward me with a slight bow and with a slow motion made with his hat, "but will you tell me who is the master of this house?"

"I am," he answered, with a smile.

"But who are you, your name, please?"

"Has no one told you? Hah, don't you know yet?" His voice conveyed a sense of injury that so important a preliminary had been overlooked.

"No one has told me."

"Then, Sir, I have the pleasure of introducing myself.   I am Giles Talcom."

"Oh, Senator Talcom."

His eyes snapped, he touched his "dab" of beard, and said:

"At your service, Sir."

We shook hands, and he sat down   "I have heard of you, Senator."

"Yes, I have introduced into the Mississippi Senate a great many reformatory measures, some of which have been adopted by our sister States."

"And you are the man who whipped Lige Patton."

"What!" he cried, snapping his eyes at me.   "Hah, you got that nonsense from old Zack Mason, the pilot.   Confound his old hide, he never will forget that.   I was quite a young man in those days, Sir.   I came here from Virginia, almost straight from the University, and was, if my examination should prove satisfactory, to take charge of a young ladies' school.   But on the day before the examination took place

Mr. Patton took it into his head to walk over me.　He didn't, and, sir, without any examination at all, the good people gave me the *male* academy.　The trustees (most of them had been river men, you understand) said that I was too valuable a piece of timber to waste on a female seminary.　They said it was too much like chasing butterflies with a bloodhound.　I didn't keep the school long; I came into my inheritance, went into politics, and here I am."

"Senator, I am under lasting obligations to you for—"

"Not at all, Sir, not at all.　I spent a very pleasant evening with you at the St. Charles Theatre in New Orleans, and I said then, as I always do when a man has entertained me, I hope to be able to do something for him.　And, Sir, while the opportunity was brought about by a sad misfortune, yet—yet I am really gratified at being the instrument, you understand, of giving you shelter and attention at this sad hour."

"How long have I been here?"

"Three days. But don't let that worry you. You are to remain until you feel perfectly able to proceed on your way."

"Were many people killed?"

"Quite a number. Two were found yesterday at the island twenty miles below. A large number were hurt, but they are being cared for. Our city is making great strides, but we have no hospital as yet, so our citizens threw open their doors to receive the wounded. And the dead have been cared for."

"How did our company fare?"

"Sir, I appreciate your modesty and unselfishness in not asking about your brethren first of all. The manager was killed, but the others escaped with slight injuries. Mr. Culpepper called to see you, but you were asleep at the time. And the old pilot, who escaped with a few bruises, has sent you his congratulations. He says that united he and you stood, and that divided you both fell."

3

"There is something else I should like to ask, about the big negro who stays here at night?"

"Oh, Washington Smith. But don't make a mistake and call him Wash. He is a humble servant of the church, but a dignified citizen of the Republic. Strange fellow. A number of years ago he presented a singular petition to the city council, begging for an education, and agreeing to work for the corporation in return for the money expended in his behalf. Most of the councilmen condemned the petition as a piece of impudence, but I was a member at the time, and I looked on it with favor, Sir. My enemies said that I was bidding for the negro vote. I raised money enough to send Washington to the Fisk University, and I can say with truth that I have never regretted the step, for he has held before me a constant example of gratitude. But I have talked to you long enough," he added, arising. "I don't want to tire you out— I want to see you on your feet again. And it won't be long. As soon as you are able to sit up we'll put you into a rocking chair, draw you into the parlor and Mrs. Estell will read to you."

He gave me a bow, accompanying the act with a slow and graceful sweep of his hat, and withdrew, leaving me to muse over the prospect of being compelled to submit to a torture administered by a Mrs. Estell. I could put up with the reading of a girl in her first poetic era, but I shuddered at the thought of a woman in her second sentimental childhood.

CHAPTER V.

A MOMENT OF FORGIVENESS.

CULPEPPER called in the after-noon, and when he saw me lying there with my head tied up, he was brusk for a moment to cover the whimper in his voice. With genuine affection he took my hand, and all the enmity I had held against him was gone in a moment. He said that the boilers of the Red Fox had blown off the end of our season, and had shattered the greatest dramatic combination that ever looked with horror at a piece of paper in the hand of a village sheriff.

"And the poor old elephant is flat on his back," I said.

"Now, here, old chap, none of that. It was only a guy. Why, we all liked you, but hang it all, Maurice, you did appear just a little stuck on yourself, not on account of your acting, but—"

"But on account of my despair," I broke in. "The nerves of my failure were exposed, and nothing is prouder than a nerve. I have told you that before I made a venture I studied for the stage, viewing it as a classic and high-born profession. I went through the best schools, and—"

"Now, here, old chap, don't talk about schools. They are only intended for society women, you know. The main trouble is, you didn't begin early enough. You were a dramatic critic and then thought you'd study for the stage."

"But my work as an actor is popular with the people," I protested.

"Yes, some people, old chap, but you mustn't pay much attention to that. In his own generation a man is not really great until the critics have pronounced him so. The critics can gradually bring the people around to an appreciation of a true artist, but popularity doesn't compel the critics to deliver a favorable verdict. It isn't with acting as it is with writing, you know. An actor is of the present, and a writer may be of the future. Wouldn't you rather have the good opinion of a few high-class men and women than the enthusiastic commendation of the rabble?"

"Yes, wouldn't you?"

"No, I wouldn't, old chap, for I am after what money there is in it. I don't expect to be an artist, you know—I don't care to be—too much hard work; too much restraint in it."

"Culpepper"—I looked at him earnestly, for I was moved by a spirit of truth—"I would rather stand high as the exponent of any art that I might choose than to have all the money you could heap about me."

"Ah, that's where you are weak, old chap; but it's well enough that there are such men—they give the other fellows a chance. And now, pardon me, Maurice, but you'll never be a great actor."

He said this with such kindliness that I did not feel even the quiver of a resentment. In fact, while left to commune with myself, and under that strange sharpening of self-judgment which illness or a nervous shock may sometimes bring about, I had seen my incurable faults and had consigned myself to mediocrity.

"Have I hurt you, old chap?"

"No," said I, philosopher enough to laugh, "you simply agree with my own estimate."

"That so? Good. But I tell you what I believe you can do, and do it down to the ground—write for the stage. You've got a good sense of humor and a first-rate conception of character; you are poetic and can soon acquire a knowledge of construction. Want me to shake on it? Of course."

We shook hands, not that he had tickled my vanity, but because he had sent back the echo which my secret mind had shouted.

"But, Culpepper, there is always a

trouble in the way. I can't work while jerked about the country—I've tried it— and just at present I can't afford to stay long enough in one place."

"That's all right, set your mind on it and the opportunity will come."

"By the way, I have a treat in store. Hope you'll be here to share it with me. I am promised a reading by Mrs. Estell, when I am able to be dragged into another room."

He laughed. "Know what I'd do?" said he. "I'd pretend weakness until the proper time, and then I'd take to my heels. Oh, by the way, I've had your trunk sent up. It fell over on the sand and wasn't injured. Say, haven't told you about Mrs. Hatch. She wasn't hurt—we were at the stern, and you must have been over the boilers. Well, she's gone on to Memphis in a rush. Old Norton telegraphed her. She sent her regards; said she was sorry she hadn't time to see you. Newspapers made a big spread of this affair. Biggest send-off we ever had. Eh? At first they had everybody killed."

He spoke feelingly of our manager, pointed out virtues that he did not possess, and forgave his inability to pay salaries. "Yes, Sir, Tabb wasn't a bad fellow," he went on. "By the by, he made a bet that he would ride home, and he has won it. Well," he said, getting up, "I leave to-night. Wouldn't go without seeing you."

He held out his hand and, taking it, I told him not to forget the "Elephant."

"Come, old chap, don't do that," he replied, assuming a bruskness, and turning about to hide his eyes from me. "You know it was only a guy. And haven't I come to tell you that you can make a great man of yourself? Well, once more, take care of yourself."

Now that he was gone, I could look back and see that Culpepper had always been a good fellow. And with a sort of pitying contempt I acknowledged that I had set myself up as a target for ridicule. But I did not merit the supercilious airs with which Miss Hatch had treated me, and to-

ward her I had not entered into a forgiving
mood, though now I know that had she entered the room while I was indulging these
reflections, I should graciously have agreed
that she, too, had always been one of the
"best of fellows."

The Senator came in just before supper-
time, bringing a newspaper, which he said
was still damp with the dew of recent
events.   He carried his soft hat in his hand,
nor did he put it down when, unfolding the
paper, he stood to catch the light at the
window.   He said that he supposed I must
be anxious to hear from the great world of
politics, and he proceeded to read an edito-
rial forecast of the election for congressman
from the state-at-large, halting to comment
upon the views set forth and making slow
gestures with his hat.   It was a local jour-
nal, but it had reproduced the political
opinions of other publications, and these
the Senator read with sharp avidity.   I
asked him if he thought he could find any
theatrical news, but he cut me off with his

hat, and gave me a paragraph on beet sugar, which he deplored as an outrage, intended to lessen the value of the plantations down the river. The light was fading, and I was not sorry. He stood closer to the window, that he might better harvest the last glimmer of the fading day, and in my cold dread of his lighting a lamp, I did not hear what he read, simply catching now and then such political frayed ends as *per capita* and *ad valorem*.

"Ah," said he, "here is a liberal extract from Tomlinson's great speech. But it's getting most too dark. Shall I light a lamp?"

I replied that I was afraid that he might tire himself pursuing his kind desire to entertain me.

"Oh, not at all, not at all, I assure you," he quickly spoke up. "But I guess you've had as much as you ought to digest at present. Feed, but don't gorge, is my motto. A hungry calf can run faster than a foundered horse. I tell you," he added, putting

the paper under his arm and coming toward
me, "there's going to be a warm election
here this fall. Of course I'm a candidate
for reëlection—the Senate couldn't get
along without me—and I don't know that
I've got but one very bitter enemy, and he is
none other than the editor of this sheet,
Sir," he said, striking the newspaper with
his hat. "For a long time he was my
friend and supporter, but he ran against me
two years ago, and I beat him so badly that
since then he has been my enemy. He is
a cur, and as sure as he lives I'll get even
with him. And as the season approaches I
expect every day to find in his paper a scur-
rilous article about me; all he wants is a
pretext. Ah, here is Washington, with
your supper."

Cutting with his hat a black scallop in
the twilight, the Senator withdrew. The
giant placed the tray of dishes upon a chair
and lighted a hanging lamp. And then he
stood in the middle of the floor, his arms
folded, looking at me.

"Won't you please sit down?" I pleaded.

"I am to be commanded, Sir," he replied, seating himself, and under his ponderous bulk the chair creaked.

"Come now," said I, "throw away your stilts and walk on the ground. I have quite enough of that on the stage."

He looked at me, slowly shutting and opening his eyes as if determined that even his wink should be deliberate. "And don't you think, Sir, that it would be well if you could say that you have had quite enough of the stage itself?"

"I don't know but you are right, Brother Washington. At any rate the stage has had quite enough of me. I am called the elephant."

"Not on account of your size, Sir?"

"No, on account of my weight."

"Ah, and the hearts of all men who know not the Lord shall at last be as heavy as the elephant."

"Very true, no doubt. I wish you'd pour this coffee for me."

He came forward with a solemn tread, poured out the coffee, and returned to the chair but did not sit down until I commanded him.

"As heavy as an elephant," he repeated, slowly winking at me.

"In working for the soul of the white man, Brother Washington," said I, "you have set about to return a good for an evil. The white man enslaved your body and now you would free his soul."

"Sir, the first shipload of negroes sent to this country was the first blessing that fell upon the Ethiopian race. In slavery we served an apprenticeship to enlightenment. Wisdom could not have reached us through any other channel. The negro was not born with the germ of self-civilization."

"You are a philosopher, at any rate."

"No, humbler, and yet greater, than a philosopher," he replied.

"All right, I'm ready to grant anything. By the way, tell me something about the Senator and his family."

"If he has told you nothing, I am at liberty to tell nothing, for, as yet, you are a stranger."

"Oh, I see. He's a shrewd politician, isn't he?"

"He is a gentleman and he is not dull. He was my friend w'en dem scoun'rels—"

I looked at him in surprise. His fall into the dialect of his brethren had come like a slap. He bowed his head, and I know that had not the blackness of his skin prevented it he would have blushed in his disgrace. He did not look up again until I spoke to him, and then he showed me a sorrow-stricken countenance.

"Don't take it so hard, Brother Washington. Such lapses must come once in a while. You remind me of an old fellow who lost his religion occasionally by swearing."

"Haw-haw," he laughed. "One in my church right now. Swore at his mule the other day and then dropped down in the corner of the fence and offered to mortgage

his crop to the Lord for one more chance.
Yas, Sah—I mean yes, Sir," he added, the
shadow of disgrace falling again upon his
countenance.   "If you have finished your
supper I will remove the dishes," he said.

"Thank you," and as he took up the tray
I continued, "And by the way, you needn't
sit with me to-night.   I don't need you; I
am not so badly hurt as they thought I was;
and, in fact, I can sleep better if left abso-
lutely alone."

"It shall be as you desire, Sir," he said,
turning upon me with a look of kindly reproach.   "But I will pray for you."

"Oh, that's all right."

He passed out into the hall, but I called
him back to the door.   "Brother Washington, I didn't mean to be flippant when I
said 'that's all right.'   I respect your sincerity."

I thought that he glanced about for a
place to rest the tray, to halt and resume
his predetermined fight against the flesh
and the devil of my unholy calling.

"Ah, shut the door, Brother Washington."

"I thought, Sir, that you had reconsidered—"

"Not to-day—some other time."

He looked at me, making no motion that I could see; but I heard the tremulous rattle of the teacup in the saucer. There was so much of pleading in his look, so much that was martyr-like in his silence, that out of pity it arose to my mind to call him back, but then came the cool though just decision that his ardent yearning was but a spirit of ambitious conquest.

"Some other time, Washington," I said, as he turned to look at me.

4

CHAPTER VI.

INTRODUCED TO MRS. ESTELL.

A WEEK passed by with no sign of a setback and one morning the doctor said that I might sit up. Brother Washington eased me into a rocking chair, and stood as if expecting me to command him to continue the work of my conversion. But I told him to sit down, a position which he always assumed in sorrow, seeming to regard it as a retreat when his spirit cried for a charge.

The Senator came in with a hearty good morning, and instructed Washington to draw my chair into the parlor. The sore trial of listening to Mrs. Estell had come. I had not seen her, had made no inquiry concerning her, but I had thought of her, and not with kindness. The pleasure of getting again into my clothes had been marred by fancy's sketch of her—sharp of voice and sour of face—a woman whose husband had willingly died, leaving her, unfortunately, to inflict man with her elocution. I wanted to sit alone and enjoy the sweet scents blown from the garden; through the window I had seen a mocking-bird alight on the top of a magnolia tree, and in silence I wanted to listen to his song. But the Senator was my benefactor. He had found me a wounded outcast, lying unconscious on the sand, and had made his mansion my hospital; and I could not lift an ungrateful finger in protest against a torture which in his belief was an act of kindness.

"Now easy, Washington," said the Senator as he held the door open. "That's it, come ahead."

The parlor was at the end of a long and lofty hall. The Senator opened the door. The chair was drawn across the threshold, and I found myself in the midst of dark, old-fashioned furniture and the portraits of

Statesmen and of ladies done by Frenchmen who had come to this country to leave a trail of art along the shores of the mighty river.

"Not too near the window, Washington," said the Senator. "About here. Now you can go about your business and I will introduce Mrs. Estell."

They left me sitting with my back toward the door. I wondered why there should be such an air of ceremony. Was it the custom in Bolanyo to dignify a torture with a stately introduction? But I had not long to muse. I heard the Senator returning. "Ah, Mr. Belford," he said, stepping into the room, "let me present you to my daughter, Mrs. Estell."

I looked round with a start, and a living line from old Chaucer, in golden letters, hung bright before me—"Her glad eyes." I bowed; and I must have spluttered my astonishment, for the Senator broke out in a loud and ringing laugh

"Sit down, Florence," he said, drawing

forward a chair for her.   And then to me, while softly laughing, he observed :

"Oh, I saw you were distressed at the idea of being read to, and I could have explained that you needn't look forward to any infliction, but I thought I'd wait and let you find it out for yourself.   Why, Sir, this child couldn't bore anybody."

"Mr. Belford, don't listen to him when he calls me a child," she spoke up.   "I am a staid married woman."

I had not, as yet, sufficiently recovered from my astonishment to venture a word, so I merely bowed, and read anew old Chaucer's glowing line.

"Yes, a child," said the Senator, "but a woman; yes, Sir, as manly a woman as you ever saw—chase a fox or shake a 'possum out of a persimmon tree.   Well, I must go down town and see what's going on.   Don't sit up too long, Mr. Belford.   Send for Washington and he'll pull you back into the other room."

"Mrs. Estell, I was never more agreeably

surprised," said I, when the Senator had taken his leave. "I expected to be tormented by an elocutionist."

"If an elocutionist is your terror, you needn't be afraid of me," she replied. "I have read to father and my husband, and that is the extent of my—shall I say, inflictions."

"Husband," I repeated. "Are you really married?"

"Surely. Why not?"

"You are so young—"

"I am not old enough to be flattered by that remark," she broke in. "Yes, I have been married two years. My husband is the State Treasurer, and is at the capital now, but will be home next week. He stays over there a good deal of the time, and I go with him once in a while, but I don't like it there. I like my old home better."

"I don't blame you for that. It must be a charming place. Have you any brothers or sisters?"

"No, Sir. It was reserved for me to be

the only and, therefore, the spoiled child. I don't remember my mother. There's her portrait."

I looked at a picture that had struck me when first I glanced at the wall. How truthfully the Frenchman had caught a sweet and gentle spirit; how exquisite was the art that had vivified those loving eyes with the speaking light of life.

"Charming," I said sincerely, and she did not look upon it as flattery, but accepted it as a truth. I looked at her and she did not avoid my eye, but met it, strong and full, with her own, and I felt that, though gentle, she was fearless. Sometimes the tone of her voice was serious and the expression of her face thoughtful, but her eyes appeared to have been always glad.

"When are you going to begin reading to me?" I asked, after we had sat for a time in a contemplative silence.

"I'm not going to read to you. Don't you see I haven't brought a book?"

"Then play something," I requested, looking toward the piano.

"I don't play; and now I must tell you, Mr. Belford, that I haven't a single accomplishment. I can't sing, and I never cared for dancing; I don't draw, wouldn't attempt to paint, and I can't speak a word of Italian. I was never intended for anything but a real companion for my father, and a dutiful wife to my husband. I am wholly unadorned."

"No, you are adorned with the highest qualities. Any woman can learn to play a piano, to speak Italian and to make an attempt at painting, but every woman cannot be a perfect companion for a man."

"And a dutiful wife to her husband," she said, laughing. "But to be dutiful is not so serious a matter.—not so serious to us as I fancy it is to you stage people."

"Well, no," I admitted; "and also more serious than the views held by thousands of good people who live in the large cities."

She shrugged her shoulders. "Nature

doesn't grant divorces," she said. "Birds are not divorced."

"But they change mates every year," I replied.

"Oh, do they? The shameless creatures."

We laughed, looking straight into each other's eyes. I thought that she would make a splendid figure on the stage, and I told her so, expecting to hear her cry out against it, but she did not. She was pleased. "I have had that sort of longing," she said, "but I never expressed it, knowing that it would meet with a storm of disapproval. It wouldn't do," she continued, shaking her head. "I know that I could never reach the top, and a lower place—"

"Would make your proud heart sore," I cried, with bitterness.

She gave me a quick look of compassion, but said nothing ; she let me continue: "I have had the cold clamps put on my impetuous soul, and, trying to conquer the evil opinion of the critic, I have worked and studied under the stimulus of despair.

But I have given up the fight; I am going to quit the stage."

I leaned toward her, hoping for a protest, but she quietly said, "I don't blame you," and I settled myself back with a sigh.   She had seen me act.

"What line of work do you intend to take up?" she inquired.

"I am going to write plays."

"And will you be satisfied if you don't write the best?"

"I hadn't thought of that.   Yes, in that line I think that I shall be satisfied with merely a success."

And then with a wisdom that made me stare at her, she said: "We can find contentment in the middle ground of a second choice, for then the heart has had its day of suffering."

"What do you read to your father?" I asked.

"Dull books in leather," she answered. "And I have sometimes feared that this schooling has unfitted me for the light and pleasing society of my friends. They called me an old maid before I was twenty. Oh, I've got something to show you," she cried, jumping up and running out of the room; and soon she returned with a little chicken held against her cheek. "A hawk carried its mother away, and all of its brothers and sisters were drowned in the rain. Listen to the little thing. Isn't it sweet? I had a pet duck once and I loved it until it got big enough to go out and get its feet muddy and then—I granted it a divorce. And after a while this little thing will grow up and leave me, won't you, pet? No, you won't, will you? There, I knew you wouldn't. You'll always be little and lovable, and will stay with me. Come on, now, and let's go back to the kitchen." She tripped out a girl, singing as she went, but she came back a woman; and of the ways, the air and the ambitions of the town I gathered more from a few moments of her talk than her father could have given me in an hour's oration. He knew the men, but she knew the whims; and while men may build the houses and make the laws, it is the whim that makes the atmosphere. And for this reason an old town is always more interesting than a new one. The subtle influence of odd characters long since gone continues to live in the air. The Spaniards had settled on the site of Bolanyo, and though naught but the faint tracings of a fortified camp were left to mark the manner of their occupation, still the town felt the honor of almost an ancient origin.

We talked until nearly noontime; until there came a light tap at the open door. I looked up and there stood the black giant.

"Pardon me," he said, "but I am afraid you have been up long enough."

"Hannibal, your unbending discipline—" I began, but with lifting his mighty hand he shut me off.

"I am a soldier of the Lord and Hannibal was a soldier of the devil," he said. "Please don't compare us."

Mrs. Estell jumped up, laughing. "You'll have to do as he tells you, Mr. Belford."

I had no time to argue against his authority, for already he had advanced and put his hands on the back of my chair. She walked beside me down the hall, and as the giant was easing the chair across the threshold of my room she said:

"I hope you'll soon get well, and when you do, we'll go fox-hunting, you and papa and I. Won't that be fun?"

"I don't know," I answered, from the inside of the room. "Oh, yes, it will be fun for you and your father."

The negro took hold of the door as if impatient to shut it, and I looked at him hard enough, I thought, to have bored him through, but, giving me simply the heed of his slow wink, he continued to stand there.

"Of course, you can ride a horse," she said; and quickly she added: "Gracious alive, Washington, don't look at me that way. Good-bye, Mr. Belford."

The negro closed the door. "Damn it,

man, what do you mean?" I cried. "Confound you, can't you see—"

"Sir," he said, standing over me with his arms folded, "do you know what you are saying?"

"Yes, I do, and I want to tell you right now, and once for all, that I appreciate your kindness, but will not submit to your insolence. Do you understand?"

"I hear you, Sir."

"But do you understand; that's the question?"

"I understand, but you don't," he said. "Now, listen to me. There is the noblest young woman in the world; when she was a child I was her horse, the black beast who delighted to do her bidding. I know her—I know she is hungry for someone to talk to. Now, do you understand?"

I did, but I said "No." I knew that she was hungry; but if I could give her food, why should this monster dash it to the ground?

"If you don't, the theatre is a more innocent place than I think it is," he replied.

I looked up at him and he winked at me slowly. "But you say she is noble," I said.

"She is, Sir, and strong; but a marriage tie cannot hold an unwilling mind. Don't misunderstand me, Sir. The greatest harm you could do would be to make her still more dissatisfied. With the presumption of an old servant, I may say something that sounds impertinent, but I am a preacher and a moralist. Thomas Rodney Estell is regarded here as a great man; he has been State Treasurer nearly ten years, and he and the Senator are warm friends."

"Well?" I said.

He looked up at the ceiling and replied: "A girl may marry her father's friend, but it is not often that she loves him."

"Washington, are you in league with the devil?"

This struck through the superficial coating of his education, into his real negro nature and made him roar with laughter. "No, Sah, I'm er feard o' him;" but feel-

ing the disgrace of his dialect he sobered
and said: "I think you understand me
now, Mr. Belford."

"Yes, I do, and I don't blame you. But
before we go further let me tell you this: I
have been on the stage, which is quite
enough to fix my character in the opinion
of many a good but narrow-minded person,
but I am from a long line of Puritan
stock, and in my blood there is a strong
sense of moral responsibility. I have never
made an intentional show of those puritanic
influences; I have striven rather to hide
them from the contempt of my lighter-
hearted companions; but a sagacious old
stage-strutter once held up my overreligous
ancestors as the cause of my failure to catch
the subtle art of a high grade of work. He
declared that all great English-speaking
actors could trace their blood back to the
cart's tail."

"I don't understand, Mr. Belford—the
reference to the cart's tail."

"To ease their consciences and to serve

the Lord with becoming activity, it was the custom of the Puritans, in the olden day, to condemn actors and tie them to the tail of a cart, and whip them through the street."

"I have never read about it, Mr. Belford."

"I suppose not. Church history doesn't dwell upon it."

He turned toward the door, faced about and said: "The woman will bring your dinner. I am going out among my people and shall not be here again until to-morrow."

"You needn't come then, Washington."

"Yes, to pull your chair into the parlor."

"That's so. Thank you."

He stood for a moment in silence, and, without speaking, he stepped back, and, with a grave nod and a slow wink, he softly shut the door.

5

CHAPTER VII.

THE NOTORIOUS BUGG PETERS.

I MENDED so rapidly that within a week I was able to walk about. Washington had every day drawn my chair into the parlor; but when I no longer was in need of this physical service, he continued his visits to give me the benefit of his spiritual strength. And once, when he came into my room, like a dark reproach, I chopped off his moral droning with the command to "get out!" He obeyed in silence, and I thought that I had given our relationship a mortal wound. But in the garden the next day he came up with unusual cheeriness and invited me to his church to hear him preach upon the strength of the Spirit and the weakness of the human family.

One day the Senator took me out in his

buggy.   He drove me through the town, and what a delight it was once more to look upon the affairs of man.   The buildings were for the most part old, and many of them were dingy from neglect, but the air was restful and romantic.   At every turn, after leaving the business center, we came upon magnolia trees, now in full bloom. Here was a garden whose low brick walls were green and gray with time, a patch of moss and a cluster of snails; and away over yonder was a blush on the landscape— a jungle of roses.   There were flowers everywhere, and far from the mansions of the lordly was many a log hut, beautiful in a tangle of vines.   We drove down the river, toward a densely timbered flat, but did not penetrate its malarious shade, the Senator choosing to turn to the left to drive me to a distant hill whereon stood the school for girls, the one of which he might have taken charge, had not his fight with Lige Patton proved him fitted for a more manly charge— the male academy.   As we were driving

along, a tall, gaunt man climbed over a
fence, stepped out into the road and sig-
naled us to stop. The Senator drew up,
laughing. The man came forward, put his
hands on the buggy tire, took them off,
"dusted" them to brush off the dirt, and
put them on the tire again. The Senator
introduced Mr. Peters, and our detainer
looked up, grinned and said :

"Yes, Sir, the notorious Bugg Peters."

His face was thin and sallow, his long
hair looked like hay, and his eyes were
simply two pale yellow spots.

"Out ridin' for your health, Senator?"

"No, just thought I'd show my friend,
Mr. Belford, the town and the country."

"Ah, hah! Oh, yes, he's one of the men
that was blowed up. And he's stayin' at
your house. Ah, hah! He's about the last
of 'em, ain't he? I heard that all that wan't
dead had put off somewhere. Never was
blowed up, that is, by a boat, but I've went
through mighty nigh everything else. Almost
hugged to death by a bear down in the cane-

brake just before the June rise eight year ago. Don't reckon your friend was ever hugged by a bear," he went on, speaking of me as if I were not there.

"No," I answered.

"Then you've got a good deal to look forward to," he replied, recognizing that, like Paul, I was permitted to speak for myself. "I've had a good many things to happen to me, first and last, but I don't know of anything worse than a bear's hug, unless it is son-in-laws."

The Senator began to laugh and I looked at Mr. Peters for an explanation. He did not keep me waiting.

"I've got seven son-in-laws down yonder in my house right now," he said, "dusting" his hands again and putting them back on on the tire. "Every time a gal of mine gits married she goes away for a few days with her husband, and then fetches him back with the ague; and he settles down in my house and there he shakes. Got seven of them down there now a-shakin' fit to kill

themselves. If you'll step over there on that
rise, you can look down in the bottoms and
see my house, and I'll bet you it's a-tremblin'
like a leaf right now. Them seven fellers
keep it a-shakin' all the time. Yes, Sir.
Now, when Mag took a man, I says, says I,
' Mag, I have always looked on you as the
smartest one of the family, and I want you
to do me a favor; I want you to see if you
can't take that feller of your'n so far away
that he can't git back.' And, Sir, I sold my
oats and give her the money, and she cleared
out, but in less than a month here she come,
with her husband shakin' like a wet dog.   I
told him to go in and find shakin' room if
he could, and he crowded his way up to the
fireplace, and there he sets this minute,
a-shakin' like a pound of calfsfoot jelly."

"Look here, Bugg," said the Senator,
laughing, "why don't you move out of the
bottoms?"

"What, and go up in the hills and ketch
some new-fangled disease that I don't know
nothin' about? I reckon not, Senator.   I've

learned to let well enough alone, and jest ordinary everyday chills is good enough for me. Mister, how long are you goin' to be with us?" he inquired of me.

"I don't know exactly. I wanted to go yesterday, but the Senator wouldn't hear to it."

"Well, I don't reckon you are able to do much knockin' about yet. Don't believe I'd be snatched, anyway. Like for you to come down to see us before you go. I can show you about the finest and shakinest set of son-in-laws you ever saw. Did think somethin' of showin' 'em at the State Fair this fall. But say, gentle*men*, you must sorter excuse me for stoppin' you; but I wanted to see the Senator on business."

The Senator gathered up the lines as if he had a suspicion of the business referred to, and therefore desired to drive on, but Mr. Peters in a distressful tone of voice implored him to wait a moment. "I want to ask a favor," he said. "Wouldn't do it if it wan't for the fact that they are all down there shakin' for dear life. I want to give you my note for ten dollars for thirty days. You know I'll take it up."

"Yes, if you should happen to find it," the Senator replied.

"Come, now, Senator, don't. talk that way. You might give this here man that was blowed up a bad opinion of me. I've got the good opinion of everybody else, and I don't want the bad respects of a man that has fell down in amongst us."

"Bugg, how many of your thirty-day notes do you suppose I've got?"

"Why, none," he declared in great surprise.

"I can show you twenty at least," said the Senator.

"Well, now," Mr. Peters began to drawl, "this here is news to me, and mighty sad news at that. Huh, I don't see how I could have made such a mistake."

"I was the one that made the mistake," the Senator replied.

"Now don't say that, Talcom. Dang

it, haven't I always voted for you? Why, Sir, at the last election I went to the polls with a chill on me, and I shook so hard it took two men to hold me still long enough to shove my ticket in. Oh, I don't deny that I might owe you a note or so—may be the addition of another son-in-law kept me from payin' it—but all my gals are married now, and I don't look for any big increase in the family till my sister and her husband come from over in Arkansas to live with me; and as they ain't well and will have to pick their way along the best they can, I'll have time to take up a half a dozen notes by the time they git here."

"What do you want with the money, Bugg?"

"Why, I need about five bushels of wheat. That's what I want with it."

"Well, here," said the Senator, taking out a notebook, "I'll give you an order on my overseer for five bushels of wheat."

"Talcom, by gosh you move me, and I am fit right now to drap a tear in the palm of your hand.   Yes, Sir, you can come nearer makin' me cry than any man I ever run across."

The Senator gave him the order, and we drove on, leaving him in the road to whine his gratitude and loudly to swear that at the next election he would vote all right, even if it should take a dozen men to hold him up.

"Why do you permit such fellows to rob you?" I asked.

"Belford, I can't help myself.   That poor wretch comes near telling the truth about his sons-in-law.   Of course, he's as shiftless as a stray dog, but he's kind-hearted and has a sense of humor that tickles me. And, after all, it doesn't seem right that I should have an abundance and that other men within sight of me should be in want." He took off his hat to wave it gracefully at a lady as she passed, and still holding it in his hand, he continued: "It's luck, Belford, nothing but luck.   I've never had any management.   I have a set of books, but half the time I don't know where I stand.

My plantation pays, not because it's well managed, but because the land's rich. I bought it, together with the house I live in, with money that was left me, and the fact that I am not compelled to scuffle for a living is no particular credit to me. It's simply luck. I've got sense enough not to reach too high. Some time ago they wanted to run me for governor, but I knew what that meant. It meant two or perhaps four years in the State House, and then relegation to the shade of a 'has been.' I like politics, I like to fight for measures, and my position as State Senator suits me exactly; and I believe I can hold it for a number of years to come. It is true that I am largely preyed upon—"

"By white and black," I suggested.

"Yes, in a measure. How are you, Uncle Gabe?" he called, bowing to an old man.

"By the notorious Bugg—and by Washington," I ventured.

"Ah, Washington is different. I give

money to his church, and he is free to come
and go as he pleases.   I was the means of
his education, and, though ignoring politics,
he controls a large negro vote.   Look out
over there, you boys, that mule might kick
you.   Aunt Sally, glad to see you (bowing
to a countrywoman who came jogging along
on a horse).   Folks all well?   All but Uncle
John, eh?   Hope he'll be out again soon."

We were far beyond the outskirts of the
town, on a rise commanding a delightful
view of groves, gardens, old houses, a fort
in ruins, the easy-going city and the river.
We passed the school for young ladies, and
the Senator waved his hat at a vision of
white and pink on the portico.   "My
daughter Florence was graduated here,"
said he.   "And, by the way, you haven't
met Estell.   He was to have come home
several days ago, but business kept him.
Florence is looking for him to-day, I believe.   Strong man, about your size—not
quite so tall.   You are a good deal of a man
when you are yourself, I take it."

"I have done pretty fair work in a gymnasium," I replied.

We turned into a broad road that led to town, and which passed the Senator's house. It was a military road, my companion said, and had been marked by the passage of old Jackson's troops.

"Senator, my obligations to you are very deep indeed, and I have refrained from saying anything—"

"Well, then, don't say anything now. It's all right. Boat blew up at the door of our city, and why shouldn't we care for the unfortunates?"

"But before going away I want to give you some sort of an expression of—"

"That's all right, Sir. There's time enough."

"No, I shall go to-morrow."

"Better wait a day or two. Have you an engagement in view?"

"No, and I shall not look for one. I have decided to quit the stage."

"Well, Sir, I don't know but you are

wise.   It must be an uncertain sort of life. But what are you going to do?"

"I am going to write plays."

"That's well enough; easy work I should think.   All you've got to do is to hatch out your plot and then stand your people around it.   And look here, Belford, there are characters enough about here to make one of the best plays you ever saw.   Why not stay here and do your writing?   The fact is, we like you, and don't want you to go away."

"But I *must* go."

"You say so, but I don't look at it that way.   Of course, if you are tired of our slow and dull city, Sir, you—"

"Tired?" I broke in.   "It is the most soothing town on the face of the earth. The days melt one into another like the mellow words of an ancient rhetorician."

"Belford, I guess you are about ready to begin work on that play," he said, laughing. "There's always a strong enthusiasm behind that sort of talk.   By the way, do you think you could take hold of an opera house and manage it?"

"Yes, I think so—I know I could. Why?"

"We appear to be getting at it, Belford. We have a very good opera house here, almost new. A man from New Orleans built it, went broke in a bigger speculation, leased it to a Dutchman who fiddled in the orchestra, and now the house is without a manager. Suppose you take it?"

"I'd take it in a minute, Senator, but the fact is, I'm broke."

"Dollars melted like the mellow words of an ancient rhetorician, eh?"

For a few moments we drove on in silence, the Senator making with his hat half-circle greetings to constituents who stood in a dooryard or who met us in the road. "Ha! Lester," he cried at a man who came along in a wagon behind a span of mules; and then to me he said: "A few years ago that fellow took it into his head that I was a little too conspicuous—I had called him a liar, or something of the sort, don't remember exactly what—and gave it out that he was going to horsewhip me. And I sent him word to buy his whip from Alf Murray, first-class harness dealer, and a friend of mine, and that I would meet him at his earliest convenience. I don't know whether he patronized my friend in the purchase of a whip, but I know that when I met him on the public square the next day he had one as long as a bull-snake. And, Sir, I believe that he had intended to hit me with it."

"What caused him to change his mind?" I inquired, with no interest in the matter.

"Why, I knocked him down, and when he was able to get up and look around again the whip was gone. Since that time we've been good friends. Now, about the opera house. You say you've got no money. Now, let me tell you what I'll do. I'll advance the money and go in as a partner. The money I am compelled to spend during each campaign is beginning to eat seriously into the income from my plantation, and I would like to ease up the pressure. My part might not be a great deal, but it would help. What do you say?"

"I could go off into all sorts of extravagances, Senator. I could say that you have made my blood leap, that you—"

"But that wouldn't be businesslike. What do you say?"

"That I snap at your proposition."

"All right, I'll go down to-morrow and rent the house."

"But you don't care to have your name known in it, do you?"

"Why not? It's all right. These people like a good show, and if we give them the best, it will make me still more useful and popular. Yes, Sir, it's all right, and we'll draw up the papers to-morrow."

6

THE STATE TREASURER.

THE town had been attractive, but now it sprung into endearment. Emotion was strong within me and my spirits rose, to find a new interest in everything and to pick up many a jest by the roadside. I caught the song of an old man who stood near the turnpike, trimming a young orchard; and the laughter of a child that was romping on the grass when we stopped at a toll gate threw sparkles of new life in the air. One sweet thrill of selfishness had made the whole world musical and glad.

"Senator, whose house is that over yonder, to the left?"

"Mine," he answered. "Oh, yes, this is the first time you've had an opportunity to view it from a distance.   We are out too far to have the advantage of gas and city water, but we've got room to swing round in, and that's worth everything.   Lumber dealer came one day and wanted to know what I'd take for those walnuts.   I told him that I'd take human life if it was necessary.   Hang me, if I didn't feel like setting the dogs on him.   I do believe," he said, shading his eyes, "that yonder are Estell and Florence.   Yes, Sir, he's got home."

At the gate, beneath the walnut trees, a man and a woman stood looking toward us. The woman was Mrs. Estell.   I had recognized her before the Senator directed my attention; I should have known her a mile away.   Her gracefulness was so original that she must have been unconscious of its effect.   The soft climate of the South had touched her with its ease, but she seemed ever on the verge of breaking away from it; and sometimes she did, not with mere gayety, but with unconquerable strength.   She enforced upon me the belief that she had taken fencing lessons.

"And suppose he should object to our compact?" was a surmise that passed through my mind; and I did not realize that I had given it actual utterance until the Senator surprised me by saying:

"None of his business. Our affair. Taking care of the funds of the State gives him about all he can look after. Helloa, there, Estell, why don't you come out to meet a fellow?"

"On the keen jump, now," Estell replied, coming slowly to meet us, his wife walking with him. It might have been the eye of prejudice that made him look so old, though why should there have been an eye of prejudice? His mustache was cropped off, stiff and gray, and his skin was thin on his cheeks and thick under his chin. The Senator introduced us, with heartiness and a flourish, and the moment I took Estell's hand I knew that from his lofty position among the money bags of the State he could not look down and find an interest in me. His nature was financial, his instincts commercial; and I can say with truth that commerce embodied in a strong and aggressive personality has always made me shudder. I am afraid of the man who delights to make figures; I feel that I am in his power. I might not hesitate to dispute with a most learned theologian, to hang with him upon the quirks of his creed, but with a pencil and a piece of paper a banker's clerk can cower me.

The Senator assisted me to alight, the Treasurer lending a pretense of his aid; and we went without delay to the dining-room where dinner was waiting. The Estells sat opposite the Senator and me; and the master of the house and his son-in-law began to talk over the affairs of State.

"Hope you had a pleasant drive," Mrs. Estell said to me.

"Charming; we had a fine view of the town, saw the old fort, and passed your college."

"Stupid old place, isn't it? But then,

it's dear, just like stupid people. Did you ever notice how dear stupid people are? They are sometimes our dearest ones. I suppose they feel that about the only thing they can do is to make themselves dear."

Estell was saying something about $246,-724, or something that sounded like that amount, but he dropped it to ask: "Florence, what are you talking about?"

"Stupid people. But you are not interested."

"No, of course not, but I was trying to get at an exact amount, and you bothered me for a moment."

"It's all right, let it go," said the Senator. "By the way, Mr. Belford and I have entered into a business arrangement. We are going to run the opera house and share profits."

Mrs. Estell cried "good." Estell gave her a look of reproof, I thought. "You mean that you are going to share losses," he said. "The thing was an elephant on Sanderson's hands."

"But it won't be on ours," the Senator spoke up. "We know how to run it. Don't we, Belford?"

"I think we do," I answered. "My fellow-players called me the manager's elephant, and in this case I don't know but we might be pitting Greek against Greek, or elephant against elephant."

Mrs. Estell laughed and so did the Senator, but Estell drank his coffee in silence. The subject was permitted to fall, but it was taken up again shortly afterward, when we had lighted our cigars in the library.

"So you think of going into the show business?" said the State Treasurer, resting his head on the back of his chair and looking up at the ceiling.

"Well, not actively," the Senator replied. "That is, I'm not to be active in the work."

"Oh, I suppose it's all right," admitted Estell; "but it's a new line and new lines are dangerous."

"But if dangerous, not without interest,"

the Senator was quick to retort. "It's settled, at any rate. I'm going to try it."

Mrs. Estell had not accompanied us. I
heard her talking to a dog in the hall, and I
listened with pleasure, for her voice was
strong, deep and singularly musical.

"The next session of the Legislature will
be a very busy one, I am inclined to think,"
Estell remarked.

"Always is," the Senator replied, laughing. "The better part of a new session is
generally taken up with the work of repeal-
ing the laws passed by an older Assembly."

I was wondering whether Estell would
ever become deeply enough interested in
my existence to warrant a straight look
from his pale and abstracted eye, when he
withdrew his gaze from the ceiling, directed
it at me and said that he was glad to see
me so far advanced toward recovery. It
was a mere commonplace which may not
have arisen from a real interest, and which
politeness could no longer defer, but it gave
me a better opinion of him.

"I suppose," said I, not knowing what else to say, "that you find your occupation one of almost painful exactness."

I think that he gave me a look of contempt. I am quite sure that, if he did not, his eye failed him of his intention.

"I wouldn't stay there ten minutes if it meant play,' he replied, and turning to the Senator he said: "Saw old Dan Hilliard the other day."

"No!" the Senator exclaimed. "You don't mean *old* Dan Hilliard."

"Yes, I do—old Dan Hilliard."

"Hanged if I didn't think he was dead. Well, I'll swear! Old Dan Hilliard! Humph! Why, I met his wife one day about three years ago and she told me that Dan was dying, that he couldn't live till night. Now what do you suppose he wanted to get well for?"

"To distress his friends, I reckon. Wanted to get five dollars from me, and said if I'd give him the money you would pay him back."

My eyes with wandering about the room alighted on two foils, crossed above a bookcase. I was right. The young woman had taken fencing lessons. And just at that moment she entered the room, a great dog following her. At the door she turned about to drive him back. He tried to spring by her; she caught him, lifted him from the floor and with a swing she tumbled him out into the hall.

"What *are* you doing?" the Treasurer cried, with a nervous jump; and the Senator, who sat facing the door, fell back with a laugh so full of contagion that I caught it before I had time to strengthen my gravity with the reflection that I might give Estell a cause to think that I was intruding myself into a family affair.

"I am teaching old Tiger to behave himself," she replied, with a smile.

"I thought you had knocked down a steer," said Estell, settling himself in his rocking chair. He shut his eyes, and to me he looked like a man who longed for rest, but who had almost despaired of finding it. "Florence," he spoke up, opening his eyes and slightly turning his head toward her, "see if you can find my slippers, please. You needn't go yourself," he added. "Send for them."

"I don't know where they are, and nobody else can find them," she replied; and hastening out, she ran up the stairs, humming an undefinable tune.

"Tom," said the Senator, "you have about worn yourself out. Why don't you go off somewhere?"

"Can't—haven't time."

"That's the biggest fallacy that man ever introduced as an economy. Did you ever know a man too busy to die?"

"No, but I sometimes think I am."

"Why don't you give up the infernal office? Nothing in it, anyway."

"Why don't you give up *your* infernal office?"

"What!" cried the Senator, and he began to run his fingers through his beard. "Now that would be a devil of a come off, wouldn't it! How is a State to get along without laws? Hah! Look at the measures that owe their origin to me. Tom, it's all right to be tired, but it's dangerous to trample on common sense. Why don't I give up my office, indeed! Now what could have put that fool notion into your head? Have you heard anybody say that I ought to give it up? If you have, out with it, and I'll make him produce his cause or eat his words. Out with it."

"Oh, I don't know that I've heard anybody say that you ought to give it up," Estell replied, opening his eyes, but closing them again before he had completed the sentence.

"You don't *know* that you have," the Senator retorted, twisting his beard to a sharp and fierce-looking point. "Estell, old fellow, there are times for joking, but this is not one of them. I make no objection to fair and honorable criticism, Sir; you know that. I grant every man the right to pass upon my acts in office—*in* office, understand; but when a man says I ought to resign, why he must show cause, or I'll stuff him like a sausage with his own garrulity. That's me, Estell, and you know it."

"Talcom, I reckon that's you. But now to be exact, I haven't heard anybody say you ought not to be in office."

"Good enough, Tom. It's all right. Yes, Sir, it's all right," said the Statesman, with no trace of his recent disquiet, but with pleasant, kindly eyes and a countenance made smooth by the justice of his cause and the pride with which he regarded his determination to defend his good name. "But, Tom, you really need rest. Oh, of course, I don't mean that you should give up public life. No, Sir," he went on, looking at me, "when a man has once been a servant of the people, he is never satisfied to fall back among the powerless 'masters.' And, Sir— of course it wouldn't do to say it everywhere, but I will say it here in confidence—I have often looked at some poor, obscure devil and have said to myself, 'Why the deuce do you want to live? You can't possibly enjoy yourself, for nobody pays any attention to you.'"

And then spoke a voice at the door. I looked around and there Mrs. Estell stood, holding a slipper in each hand, her arms hanging limp. I did not catch the words she uttered first, but these I heard and always shall remember: "And perhaps he has a wife who worships him, and children that think he's a god. And if I were a man I would rather be in his place than to have a world of flattery."

With a swift step and a graceful bend she laid the slippers at her husband's feet. The Senator clapped his hands and so did I, but Estell neither moved nor opened his eyes until he heard the slippers tap upon the floor, and then he turned his head to say, " I'm much obliged to you."

And at that moment she broke away from the soft and dignifying influences of a Southern atmosphere; she sprang upon a chair, snatched the foils from the wall, laid one of them across my knees, sprang back and with mock tragedy cried, ''Defend yourself.'' But before I could get out of my astonishment to say a word, and as the dull eyes of her husband looked up sharp with surprise, she bowed with a condescending grace and with mimic magnanimity threw down the foil and said: ''Ah, I forgot. You are wounded and a prisoner.''

The Senator looked on with pride; his face glowed and his eyes snapped, but Estell grunted: ''Mr. er-er-Belford,'' he began, again becoming vaguely conscious that I was on the face of the earth, ''the Senator had no son; and that explains why he made a tomboy of his daughter.'' He laughed weakly as he said this, and as a piece of good humor it was a failure, but it proved to me that he was not wholly ill-natured.

''That's all right,'' the Senator replied, with his eyes on Mrs. Estell, who had again mounted a chair to replace the foils on the wall. ''That's all right, but her tomboyishness has made her decidedly human, and, Sir," he added, as the young woman stepped down, "I guess she succeeded in winning the love of one of the best men in the State. Eh. How's that, old fellow?"

"Not quite so bad as I expected," Estell answered, rousing up. "You could have studied longer and framed it worse. By the way, Mr. Belmont—"

"Belford," his wife suggested, standing with her hands resting on the back of his chair.

"Yes, thank you. But, by the way, Mr. Belford, where are you from, Sir? I take it that you are not a Southern man."

"I was born near the old city of Chester, England," I answered. "But I came to this country when a boy. And among Americans I sometimes assert that I'm English, but among Englishmen I am often proud to say that I am an American."

"Good enough," said the Senator. "First rate. That's all you need to say around here, Sir. Our most famous orator,

S. S. Prentiss, used to say, when re-proached with the fact that he was not born in Mississippi, that any fool could have been born here, but that he had sense enough to come to the State of his own accord. Belford, we've had some great orators. We've had men, Sir, that could make you laugh at your own sorrow and .then compel you to look with grief upon your own laughter. But they are gone, Sir." He got up and stood with one hand thrust into his bosom. "They are gone, and the world will never look upon their like again. Why, Sir, Prentiss, with his oration on starving Ireland, made the whole world weep. Ah, and who makes it weep now? It does not weep, for there is a measure of relief in tears. It groans, and in a groan there is no sentiment—the groan is the language of despair. The oppress-ive corporation, the heartless money grabber —but I won't talk about it," he broke off, sitting down and running his fingers through his beard.

7

"Yes, it's bad," Estell drawled, "but what are we going to do about it, heigho?" he yawned. "You people may discuss the ills of the world, but I'm going up-stairs and take a nap."

CHAPTER IX.

PUBLIC ENTERTAINERS.

EARLY the next day the Senator and I went down to look at the opera house. It was about midway in a block that faced the public square. Of course there was nothing attractive in its outward appearance, and I expected to find a raw interior, but I was more than happily surprised. The auditorium was well appointed, the chairs were of the best and the decorations were modest and artistic. I felt that it was only the poorest of management that could have brought about the financial failure of the house. And now that I had seen the place there arose a fear that the agent might set the price too high. But when we called upon him the Senator explained with so many gestures intended to depress him, and with so many shrewd words thrown out to convince him that we came as benefactors, that he soon was willing to accept our terms.   The papers were drawn up at once.

"And, now, by the way," said the Senator, "I don't want to be known in this transaction, for, come to think it over, there are many people in my senatorial district who hold a prejudice against the show business.   So I'll be a silent partner, and a mighty silent one, I want you to understand."

The agent said that he understood, and the Senator continued: "The editor of that mongrel sheet, the *Times*, would twist this thing out of all shape, Sir.   He would fight the house to injure me, and he'd jump on me to hurt the house.   Mr. Belford here will be the manager, and I guess he knows all about it."

I was forced to tell him that I was not a business man, that I could secure the attractions, but that he must see that the books were kept properly. "That's all right," he said. "I can't do it myself, but I'll take them home and turn them over to my daughter. She may not know how to keep them in the regular way, but you may gamble that they'll be kept right."

I agreed to this, but as we were going out the thought occurred to me that Estell might object.

"Oh, that will be all right," the Senator declared when I spoke of it. "He may not be taken with the idea, but it will give Florence a practical thing to think about, and he can see that it will be good for her."

"But if it's just the same to you, Senator, I'd rather you wouldn't speak to him about it when I'm present. Even the slightest objection on his part would be embarrassing to me."

"You are right, Belford, and I appreciate your sensitiveness. Yes, Sir, you are right. But he won't object."

As we drew near to the house we saw Estell standing under a walnut tree. "Go on in," said the Senator, "and I will have a talk with him. It's a matter of no importance, you understand. We can hire a man to keep the books. But I'll speak to him."

I passed on into the library. The dog, that had presumed to disobey the mistress of the house, lay stretched upon the floor, and as I entered he looked up contemptuously, and then to all appearances resumed his nap. Presently Mrs. Estell came in.

"You are back early," she said. "What are you doing here?" This was spoken to the dog. He raised his head and gave her an appealing look. "They want you out there to catch a chicken to send to a sick man."

The dog brightened, jumped up and trotted out, and soon a squawk and a command from a negro woman announced that he had done his work.

"It is all arranged," I said.

"I knew it would be," she replied. "My father gets nearly everything he goes after."

"And he is now after Mr. Estell, to get his consent—"

"Consent!" she broke in. "Consent about what?"

"Why, the Senator thought it would be a good idea to bring the books up here and let you keep them."

"I'd like that. It would give me something to think about."

"That's what your father said."

"Oh, and he's gone to ask Mr. Estell. He won't care. He may object at first—he objects to nearly everything at first."

"I don't believe he takes to me very kindly," I ventured to remark.

She laughed. "Oh, he doesn't take to anyone at first. I had known him ever since I was a child, and I was grown before he appeared to think anything of me. But he doesn't seem a bit like his old self. He used to be lively and liked to go out, but now he's worried all the time and doesn't care to go anywhere. I don't know what's the trouble with him, I'm sure. Isn't that a pretty little theatre? And what do you think of the prospects? Don't you think they're good? I do."

"So do I. The town is large enough, and I believe we can make the venture pay."

"I'm sure of it," she said. "It has never been managed properly. None but the poorest plays came here, and no wonder it failed. I do hope it will be a success. It will give father something new to talk about. I'm so tired of politics. Always the same thing, anxiety and treachery and everything unpleasant. Mr. Estell was offered an excellent place in a New Orleans bank, some time ago, and I begged him to take it, but he wouldn't. And I can't understand why. There's no money and no particular honor in the place he has now. But you would think his life depended on it. He had strong opposition at the last election, and I thought he'd go wild. Here they come."

The Senator slyly winked at me as he

entered the room. But Estell did not appear to see me until he had sat down, and then he looked at me and said:

"You and Talcom are trying to involve the whole family in that show enterprise, eh?"

"We'd like to involve the whole community in it," I answered.

"Yes. And it would be a nice thing for a friend to meet me and say: 'Helloa, Estell, understand your wife, the former belle of Bolanyo, is keeping books for a show.'"

"If you object, Mr. Estell," I began, but he shut me off.

"Object? Why, I don't object to anything that Talcom does. What's the use? Oh, it's all right. And I suppose we'll have show bills pasted up all over the house. Might take a few of them to Jackson with me and stick 'em up in the Treasurer's office; might get the Governor to put up a few in the Executive Chambers. And

I know the walls of the Senate will be lined with them."

I was about to say something in resentment of this dry ridicule when the Senator looked at me with a comedian's squint of the eye. "Oh, yes," said he, "and we'll have the Governor issue a proclamation commanding all the State officers to attend our performances. By the way, he is a bachelor. We'll marry him to a—"

"Soubrette," I suggested, to help him out. The Senator laughed and Estell chuckled wearily as his wife, in her good humor, shook his chair. Dating from this trifling incident the Treasurer appeared to like me better; at least, he paid me more attention, and at dinner he told a joke (which the Senator afterward informed me was his favorite bit of humor), and I laughed as if I really enjoyed it. I felt more kindly toward him, but the eye of prejudice made him old, for constantly I wondered how she could ever have given her consent to marry him. I had been told, by the Senator, I think, that his family was high, that his people were once of the great and lordly set of the South, and of course I knew that in the marriage arrangement the name of family meant more than mental or physical suitability; and yet I could not rid myself of the belief that a violence had been committed against sentiment the day she gave her hand to her father's friend.

After dinner the Senator and I went into the library to talk over our venture, and Estell trod heavily up the stairs to take his nap. I wondered whether his wife were coming with us. She did not; she went out into the magnolia garden; and through the window I watched her as she walked about beneath the trees. To me she was such a picture, so lithe a piece of Nature's art, that in my study of her I did not think of a danger that might lie in wait for me; but in matters that tend to lead the heart astray we rarely think until too late and then each thought is an added pain.

The Senator was saying something and I looked around at him. "Yes, Sir, I think we'll run all right. Bound to if we put our energies into it. Let's see; you'll have to go North and book the attractions, won't you?"

"Yes, I ought to, but it's now almost too far along in the season. It would involve considerable expense, and I think that the best plan is to do my best with correspondence and take it in time next year."

"Shouldn't wonder but you are right. Yes, and that will give you time to work on your play. It will be quite a feather in our cap to have a play written by our manager."

"Yes, a successful play," I replied.

"Oh, don't you worry about that. We'll make it a success all right enough, for we've got the characters here under our gaze."

"And the notorious Bugg Peters is one of them," I suggested.

He began to run his fingers through his beard. "Well, I don't know about that,

Belford. It doesn't seem to me, though, that we ought to mar a play with as trifling a fellow as he is. Why, that fellow is no account on the face of the earth! Why, he's common! And, Sir, the people wouldn't go to see a play that had him in it. We can get better material, honorable and upright men, Sir. Why, he'd take all the dignity out of it; he'd bring ridicule on the South. By gracious, Sir, they'd think that he's—he's real!"

"Well, but isn't he?"

"Oh, in a way, yes. But he's not a representative man, you understand; and I want to tell you, Belford, that the stage is in need of representative men. Why, Sir, every newspaper is talking about the elevation of the stage, the need of it, mind you; and I don't see how you can elevate the stage if you put such men as Bugg Peters on it. Why, confound his hide, do you know there's not a bigger liar in this State? And do you know that he owes me?—well, I won't attempt to say how much. We'll give him wheat, Sir, to keep him and his shaking sons-in-law from starving, but we cannot—I repeat—we cannot put him on our stage.　It's nothing to laugh at, Belford. It's a serious matter.　I'll show you some characters—I'll find them for you.　Why, here's Washington.　Come in, come in."

The preacher came forward and stood gravely looking down upon us.　"Sit down," said the Senator.　"That is, unless Mr. Belford objects," he added, looking at me

"Why should I object?" I asked, in surprise.

"Oh, some people object to—"

"A negro sitting down in the presence of white gentlemen, unless he drops his hat at the door and then sits on a trunk or a box," Washington spoke up, smiling.　"But," he added, "the Senator is more liberal. However, I do not wish to sit down.　I have come on an important errand."

"Ah, ha!　How much do you need?" the Senator inquired.

The preacher roared with as genuine a

laugh as ever was blown across a cotton field.

"We don't need so very much," he said, his gravity returning with a suddenness that made him appear almost ridiculously solemn. "We need something, however, and when our own resources had fallen short, I told my brethren that I knew where to come. The truth is, we need a new bell for the church, and lack twenty-five dollars of having enough to pay for it."

"A new bell! Why, what's the matter with the old one?"

"It is cracked, Sir."

"Cracked! Why I'll bet a thousand dollars you can hear it fifteen miles. Why don't you take the money that a bell would cost and give it to the poorer members of your congregation?"

"The poor we have with us always, Senator. We need a new bell."

"Yes, and you'll ring it at all times of night and keep me awake. Why do they have to be rung, too, so much? Hang me, if I don't believe you've got one old fellow over there that gets up and rings it in his sleep; and many a time I've felt like filling his black hide with shot.   When do you want the devilish thing?"

"You mean the bell, Sir?"

"Yes.   When do you have to get it?"

"It has been ordered and it must be paid for on its arrival."

"Oh, you've ordered it.   Well, now, if you hadn't ordered it you'd never 've got a cent out of me.   Don't believe I've got that much money about me," he added, stretching out his leg and thrusting his hand into his pocket, to draw forth a roll of bank notes; and on beholding this great display of wealth the negro's thick eyelids snapped.   "Here you are," said the Senator, giving him the sum required.   "And you tell that old fellow that if he rings the new bell in his sleep, he'll wake up with his black hide full of shot."

"Thank you, Senator. You mean Brother Sampson, Sir?"

‘‘Hah? Sampson? I don't know his name, but I guess Sampson's about right. Wait a minute. Mr. Belford is going to remain with us. He is going to take charge of the theatre here, and in going about the neighborhood you may tell the people that we are—I say we because I want to see the town well entertained—tell the people that they are to have a series of the finest entertainments ever known in this part of the country. And, by the way, Belford, I forgot to speak of it, but you'd better board here at the house.’’

I looked up to meet the negro's eyes; a stare of blunt rebuke, as if the proposal had come from me, in violation of a compact made with him. I caught a vision of Mrs. Estell as I had seen her through the window, walking beneath the magnolia trees; I heard the warning voice of reason, and I saw lurking in ambush the sweetest and perhaps the deadliest of all dangers. I had seen much of the immorality of life, of passion that knew no law, but not for a moment did there live in my mind a suspicion that this woman could forget the exacting demands of a matron's duty.   I felt that the danger lay for me alone; that the warm and sympathetic relationship of friend of the family and partner of the father would establish me almost as a member of the household; that a sisterly regard would at most define the depth of the interest that she could take in my affairs, and even this must come with slow and almost unconscious ripening.   It was true that I had come a stranger, that an old community, and especially in the South, is skeptical of a new man's respectability, but I had fallen helpless upon their hospitality, and my misfortune was stronger than an introduction.

It did not seem that I had time to reason as I sat there encountering the gaze of that black agent of a moral code; my reflections might have come like flying splinters, but as I look back and again bring up the scene, I feel that they must have fallen as one impression, a cold and benumbing weight.

"It will be a long walk out here for Mr. Belford, and he has not regained his strength," the negro said, still gazing at me.

"Nonsense!" the Senator replied. "He will be as strong as a buck in a day or two, and, besides, he is used to his room out here and might as well keep it. Confound your impudence, Washington, you always oppose me."

"I beg your pardon, Senator."

"That's all right, but I'm going to have my own way about my own affairs. Do you understand?"

"Better than you think, Sir."

"What's that?"

"I mean that I understand perfectly."

"Well, say what you mean."

"Senator," said I, "he is right. I'd better get a room down town. Walking in and out—and I couldn't think of riding—would take up too much of my time, and I expect to be very busy after the season opens."

"Well, now, there may be something in

that.　　Yes, Sir, there's a good deal to be attended to.　Suit yourself.　Perhaps it would be better.　Washington, you go on and pay for your diabolical arrangement to keep me awake."

The negro bowed and gave me a look, but not of victory—of gratitude.

CHAPTER X.

MR. PETTICORD.

EARLY the next day I was formally installed as manager of the Bolanyo Opera House. The Senator directed the ceremony, marking long meter with his hat, and by his solemn mien appearing to demand of me a serious and majestic chant, the tune of Old Hundred, to express a deep sense of my responsibility—a mere fancy, of course; but as a matter of fact, he did seem to believe that we ought to make a sentiment of this commonplace and businesslike procedure. But I told him that we would wave the rights of a mysterious incantation and look upon the affair as a commercial transaction.

"Yes, of course," he said. "But you know there has always been a sort of mystery about the stage. It holds us to the past, makes us children, afraid of ghosts. It has a peculiar smell; and one thing about it is, that all the people on the stage seem to be foreigners, it makes no difference how well you may have been acquainted with them. I don't know that it's true in all cases. Come to think of it, you don't seem strange to me."

"There has always been a prejudice against the stage, in England and America," I replied. "Our race cannot associate art and religion, when, in fact, there's true religion in every phase of art."

"Well, now, I don't know about that, Belford. The Pagans worshiped idols and some of their idols were works of art, but there was no true religion in that. But be that as it may, we're going to make a success of this thing."

A number of boys, having scented an unusual activity, were hanging about the door, and one of them made bold to ask if there was going to be a show.   The Senator answered him. "Yes, there is, my little man, and we'll want you to take around some bills when it comes, next fall. Whose son are you, anyway?"

"Mr. Vark's."

"Oh, yes, the shoemaker down stairs. Well, run along now."

The boys scampered off, and the Senator, looking about, declared that we were making great progress. "Yes, Sir, we'll coin money here; and do you know, Belford, I am beginning to believe that money is a pretty good thing after all? Yes, Sir, I have about arrived at that conclusion. It won't take a man to Heaven, but it arms him against a hell on earth. Let me see, there was something else I intended to say. Oh, yes. Now it's all right to be friendly with everybody, but intimacy is a dangerous thing. Encourage it and the first thing you know the loafers about town will begin to call you by your first name. That kills a man if he's in any sort of public life. Why. Sir, if I had let those fellows call me Giles,

I couldn't have remained in the Senate more than one term; would have killed me, Sir, as dead as a door nail. In this human family a man thinks more of you in the long run if you compel him to bow to you than if you permit him to put his arm on your shoulder. Our natures respect exclusiveness. We may make fun of what we conceive to be a groundless dignity, but at its face we bow to it. Well, you can now begin your correspondence. I have put money to your credit at the bank, and there's nothing to keep you from going ahead. There are some other little details. that can be arranged at our leisure. And now, as to a boarding place. Our hotels are not first class. And here's what I regard as a good idea. This room off here you can fit up as a sleeping apartment, and you can take your meals at a restaurant. Suit you?"

"Perfectly. And I want to thank you for your—"

"Wait till the end of next season, Sir;

we haven't time now. And, by the way, I want you to come out to the house as often as you can conveniently. Just come and go as you please. Well, Mr. Manager, I'll bid you good-morning."

My room was airy, and, proportioned in that wastefulness of space which marks one of the interior differences between the town and the great city, it afforded the luxury of many an imaginary path over which I could walk in meditation upon my play; and that piece of work was uppermost in my mind. It was my hope to exist as a manager until I could pip the shell as a dramatist—selfish, I confess; and so is art a selfishness, and so is every high-born longing in the breast of man. Indeed, philanthropy itself cannot escape the accusation: To give to the needy awakens the applause of the conscience.

A slight tapping attracted my attention, and looking round I saw standing in the doorway a tall, gaunt man with a beard so red as to shoot out the suggestion that it had been put on hot and that sufficient time had not elapsed for it to cool.   I invited him in; and, stepping forward, he handed me a card on which in black type and with heavy impression was printed the name Lucian C. Petticord, followed by the information (also heavy and black) that I was in the presence of the Editor of the Bolanyo *Daily Times*, and the enemy of Senator Giles Talcom.

"Sit down, Mr. Petticord.   Glad to meet you," I added, with lie number one.

"Thank you," he said, seating himself. "Match about you?"

I found a match for him, and lighting the stub of a cigar, he said "Thanks," crossed his legs and hooked his thumbs in the arm-holes of his "vest."

"How do you like our town?" he asked.

"Charming place," I answered.

"Used to be, but hard times hit it a crack and it's been staggering ever since. Had two banks—one of them failed.   Tough, I tell you, but we'll come out all right. Just heard of your deal.   Ought to make the thing pay, I should think.   Got to spend some little money, of course.   By the way, is old man Talcom interested in it?"

"Well, only as a friend," I answered, with lie number two.

"I heard he was.   Always was a sort of a theatrical fellow."

"He is a gentleman, if that's what you mean."

"Yes, in a way," he drawled.   "Oh, I know him."

"Then, Sir, you know one of the most generous of men."

"Yes, generous in a way.   Pretty keen, though—he's not throwing anything over his shoulder this year, and he didn't last year either, for that matter."

"I didn't know," said I, "that throwing a thing over one's shoulder was esteemed as an example of generosity."

He rolled his cigar about between his fiery lips.   "I take it that you know what I mean," he replied.   "I mean that Brother Giles ain't giving anything away without cause."

"Who is?" I asked, and I looked at him hard, but, in the vernacular of the neighborhood, I did not "faze" him.

"In general, nobody; and in particular, not Brother Giles. Well, it's all right. Glad he ain't interested financially. Presume, however, he advanced you the necessary money."

"Pardon me, but if he did it doesn't concern you."

"Oh, it's all right; no business of mine except as a matter of news."

"But what doesn't concern the public is not news," I replied.

"No, that's a fact, but then, there comes up a difference of opinion as to what does concern the public." He paused for a few moments and then continued: "Thought I'd step over and see if I could get an ad from you. Do all my own work in that line; do all the editorials and write most of the local leaders. It keeps me busy, but I'm getting out the best paper the city ever had.   And my ad rates are not high when the circulation is considered."

"I shall give you an advertisement later on," said I, "but just at present there could be no object in it.   It's out of season and there's nothing to advertise."

"But you'll want a write-up announcing the change of management.   The people will be interested in it, you know."

"Yes, but doesn't that very fact make it a piece of legitimate news?"

"Well, yes, in a way.   But you know I can't afford to print news for nothing.   I'm not printing news for my health, you know. Write you up in good shape for ten dollars."

It was the easiest way out of what appeared to be the beginning of an unpleasant entanglement, and I told him that he might proceed with his "write-up."   It was a sort of bribery, the purchase of his good opinion in the hope of securing his silence, for I knew that there must be war, and perhaps a complete change of geographical lines, so far as I was concerned, if the newspaper should offensively associate the Senator and the playhouse. But as I sat there, the subject of a "pleasant interview"—meeting smile with smile—I actually ached to kick that red gargoyle down the stairs.

"Well," he said, blowing the cigar stub out of his mouth and letting it fall where it might, "I'll get back to work. Come over sometime."

"Thank you. I may see more of you when the season opens."

"Guess that's right. Haven't got a cut of yourself, have you?"

"No, and I don't care for one."

"You're wrong there; good cut's a first-rate thing—catches the women, and I want to tell you that unless you catch the women you don't catch anybody. Well, good day."

Almost as soothing as a melody was his passing footstep down the stairs. But he halted, and I heard him talking to someone who evidently was coming up. I was afraid that he had turned to come back, and I stood in a tremor of dread, when in stepped old Zack Mason, the steamboat pilot. "Hah, united we stood and divided we went up!" he cried, grasping my hand. "How are you?—first-rate, I know. Oh, this climate will bring a man out of the kinks if he isn't killed instantly. All this atmosphere needs is a few minutes' start. A man can grow a set of new lungs down here. How are you, anyway? Didn't hurt me much—made a trip since then on a snag-boat. Tickled to death to see you again. How are you, anyway?"

During all this time he held me with a grip so tight as to assure me that not even an explosion could blow us apart. And whenever I attempted to tell him how I was, or to impress him with my share of the pleasure derived from our meeting, he gripped me tighter, to hold me under the outpour of his congratulations. "Felt like a brother had left me that day when you were snatched out of my hand. Said to myself, as I flew through the air, 'he's got a little bit the start of me and I don't believe I'll ever see him again.'　And last night, when I got home and heard you were around all right, I went straight over to old Jim Bradley's and swallowed a drink as long as a pelican's neck.　I want to tell you that Jim's got the stuff right there in his house—been here ever since the Mississippi River was a creek; and he's got licker older than Adam's off ox.　And I'll tell you what we'll do this minute—we'll go right over there and take a snort as loud as the sneeze of a hippopotamus."

By this time I had forced him back into his chair, but he showed such a keenness to get at me again that I had to remind him that I had been but a short time out of bed.

"Well, now, I'd about forgotten that," he declared.　"But I don't want you to handle me after you get plum back at yourself.　You are as strong as a panther right now.　But that's neither here nor there. The question is, will you come over with me to see old Jim?　I've got a lay-off for about a week, and I've got to have a little fun as

I go along.   Eat, drink and be merry, for to-morrow you may be blowed up.   And we'll see old Joe Vark over there.   Joe's got a shoeshop right down here—best shoe-maker that ever pounded the hide of a steer —works till he gets ready to have fun, and then he whoops it up.   He's smarter than a serpent, even if he ain't always as harmless as a dove.   They started a little public library here once, and the first thing they knew old Joe had nearly all the books stacked up in his shop; and he read them, too.   Come on and we'll go down to old Jim Bradley's; and he's all right, too.   What do you say?"

"To tell you the truth, I'd rather go with you than to do almost anything; it would fit me like a glove; but I can't.   I've had to quit.   One drink would mean a spree, and that would ruin everything."

"Yes, but here," he insisted, "the liquor that Bradley keeps won't put a man off on a spree.   It's a fact.   It would take a man two weeks to get drunk on it, and by that time he'd have enough.   Come on."

9

"No, I can't go."

"Well, if you can't drink without taking too much I'm the last man in the world to persuade you. Glad to see you, anyway. And I reckon you're going to give us a first-rate line of shows. Met the Senator just now and he told me. He's another man that can't drink. I can drink and I can let it alone—that is, I know I can drink, and I think I can let it alone. Well," he said, getting up and taking my hand, "I'm glad to have seen you again, anyway. Take care of yourself, and when your first show opens up I'll come round with the boys and we'll whoop things up."

CHAPTER XI.

THE CHARM OF AN OLD TOWN.

THE spiritual atmosphere of Bolanyo was like the charm of an old book that we prize only for the almost secret art of its expression, an art too ethereal to be caught and inspected. Sometimes it was drowsy, with all the dreamy laziness of a hamlet in the south of Spain, but there were days when it seemed to rebel against its own ease and unconcern, when a sense of Americanism asserted itself to demand a share in the bustling affairs of noisy commerce. Court day was a time of special activity. It was then that the local market felt a stimulating thrill. My window looked out upon the public square, a macadamized space, white and dazzling in the sun. Sometimes the scene was busy and interesting in variety; wagons loaded with hay still fragrant of the meadow; a brisk horse trotted up and down in front of an auctioneer; negroes with live chickens tied in bunches; a drunken man making a speech on the wretched condition of the country; a "fakir" on the corner selling a soap that would remove a stain from even a tarnished reputation.

Life along the levee was ever interesting to me, for it was there that I could study the slowly vanishing type of boatmen, once so distinctive as to threaten the coming of a new and haughty aristocracy. Singing the song of long ago, with their eyes fixed upon the river, the old negroes stumbled over the railway track that a new progress had thrown across their domain. Great red warehouses were falling into decay, and rank weeds were growing in the bow of a half-submerged steamer that years ago had won a great race on the river. Everywhere lay the rotting ends and broken ravelings of the past, but nowhere, not even in the oddest corner, could there be found the thread of a hope for the future. The business interests of the town had grown away from the river, leaving it to melancholy poetry and to death. And here I loitered, day after day, in a vague contentment extracted from a distress more vague. To a thoughtful mind there is more of interest in decay than in progress; the "Decline and Fall" is a greater book than could have been written on the "Origin and Rise."

I could find no one to tell me much of the history of Bolanyo; no one appeared to take an interest in that part of its existence which lay behind the halcyon and now almost holy day of the steamboat. I knew that, in a corrupted form, it retained the name given originally to the Spanish fortification. But that was enough to know, for the exact dates of the historian might have made it, in comparison with places of real antiquity, a toadstool of yesterday.

I saw the Senator nearly every day, in the office or on the street. Election was not far

away, and he had begun to mingle more
freely with the people; and though his
manner was as cordial and as solicitous as
on the day when driving with me he had
saluted everyone whom he met in the road,
he was far from being familiar, and no one,
except his most intimate friends, presumed
to call him Giles.

The sight of his house, pillared and
stately, on the summit of the graceful rise,
was always a pleasure, and while strolling
about, with no intention of calling (having,
doubtless, called the day before), I kept it
in view, for my eyes were never weary with
looking upon it, so white and peaceful.   It
was not a palace, not really a mansion, and
in the rich communities of the North it
would not have been noteworthy except as
a sort of quaint renaissance in home build-
ing, but to me it had not been set there by
the hand of man, but by the Genii of the
Lamp.

Upon calling one afternoon, I was told
by the negro woman that the Senator was

asleep, and, not wishing to have him disturbed, I walked out into the garden, where Washington was at work among the flowers. With the instinct of his race, he was humming a tune, and he did not hear me until I spoke to him, and then, uplifting his hand with a sign of caution, he pointed at a tree not far away. My eyes leaped to follow him, for I felt that the young woman was near, and there on a bench she sat, her head against the tree, her hat on the ground—asleep.

"Don't make a noise," he said, in tones but little louder than a whisper. "Sarah, the colored woman there in the house, say —says the young lady didn't sleep hardly at all last night, and she went to sleep out there just now."

"She isn't ill, is she?" I asked.

"Sick? No, Sir, she is well, but she's got to sleep some time. How do you like my flowers?"

"They are very beautiful."

"Yes, Sir, but don't talk quite so loud.

Seems to me like you are trying to wake her up. I didn't want to take money for this work," he went on, bending over and pulling up a weed, "for I like to do it, but they insist on paying me. Yes, Sir. And I reckon—I suppose we have here the finest clump of magnolias in all this part of the country. This one, right here, was set out the day Miss Florence was born, twenty-four years ago, now."

"And it is the most graceful tree of them all," I replied.

He cut his black eyes at me. "Yes, Sir, I believe it is, but, even if it wasn't, you might say it was. I beg your pardon, Sir, but you just as well board here. Oh, all the whole human family is not blind. If the rest of them are, I'm not."

"Look here, Washington."

"I'm looking, Sir," he said, his eyes full upon me.

"You were very kind to me, and I am grateful, but I don't want your guardianship, and I won't have your insinuations."

''Why, bless you, Sir, I don't want to be your guardian, and I don't intend to insinuate. I spoke to you once about a danger, and I was afraid you had forgotten it. Don't misunderstand me. I believe you are an honorable man, but honor is not always careful enough when it comes to talking to a lady, and none but an honorable man could make trouble on this occasion. The only trouble you can make—there (nodding toward the bench whereon the young woman sat, in fluffy white), the only trouble you can cause there," he repeated, ''would be to make her still more dissatisfied with life. And a trouble might fall hard on you, Sir. Let me tell you something in confidence. People have said that my wedding to the church was what kept me from a marriage of the flesh. I let them believe so, but it is not true. Mr. Belford, a soul that is now cool and quiet in this black breast was once raging and on fire. It was a long time ago. I had

just begun to preach.   I lived at the house
of a friend—over yonder."

He waved his hand toward a distant hill
on which was clustered a negro settle-
ment.

"And there was a woman with a face
like cream when the cow has eaten the first
buds of the clover; and her eyes were as
bright as the star that hung above the
manger, and her laugh was as sweet as the
notes that dripped like honey from the harp
of David."

He stood erect, a pose of black dignity,
his arms folded on his breast, and in one
hand he held the weed that he had uprooted
from among the flowers.   I did not question the sincerity of his religious zeal; from
what I had heard and from what I had seen
of him I was persuaded that with honesty
he had dedicated his life to the service of
his creed, but now I felt that he was making a conscious picture of his sentiment and
his sacrifice.   The bigotry of applauded
self-righteousness was in the look that he

bent upon me, and my blood rose in resentment, but I said nothing; I let him proceed.

"This woman was a wife, beyond my reach, and I felt that there was no danger for me, and therefore I was not careful, but the first thing I knew I was called upon to choose between the spirit of the Lord and the flesh of the devil."

"Washington, you are talking what is popularly known as rot. How can you compare a handsome woman with the flesh of the devil?"

"The devil's flesh may be beautiful, Sir; and beautiful flesh may not be conscious that it was laid on by the devil."

"But if the devil can tint the flesh and make it beautiful, he is an artist."

"Yes," he said, "and the devil might arm an agent with a paint brush."

"More rot, Washington. The beautiful things are of the Lord and not of the devil. The devil may have made the weed you hold in your hand, but the flowers belong to God."

With a shudder he dropped the weed, as if suddenly it had burnt him. "Well, the end of your love story; how did it come out?"

"It made the woman dissatisfied with the cold clod she was living with; and if I had not let my duty rule me there might have been a scandal, and then my day of usefulness would have been gone."

"Yes; I suppose that a preacher must necessarily look upon a woman as a sort of trap door. He may recover from the disgrace of wine, but woman—" I glanced toward the bench, to find Mrs. Estell engaged in the very human act of rubbing her eyes. I did not wait to finish the sentence, but stepped off briskly; and, looking round before she recognized my coming, I saw that Washington had dropped his dignity and was bending among the flowers. She was not startled when she saw me; she did not even show surprise, for my odd-hour presence had become commonplace.

"I'm glad you came," she said in quiet

frankness, and with a smile of welcome. "Sit down.   Isn't it a sleepy day?"

"Yes.   And even the soft air is gently snoring among the leaves," I replied, rather pleased with the fancy.

"Don't talk that way," she said. "You'll put me to sleep again." She turned her face away to hide a yawn.   "Have you begun work on your play?"

"Well, yes, I have taken some very important steps.   Day before yesterday I got some paper, got a pint of ink yesterday, and I expect to get a box of pens to-day."

"Oh, you are making great progress. You are going to let me read it, I suppose?"

"Yes, after I've had it typewritten."

"Oh, I won't want to read it then—all the character of the work will be gone—I couldn't find any of your moods and troubles in it; couldn't tell where it was easy nor where you got stuck.   I always think that handwriting holds something for me alone, but a typewritten thing is intended for everybody.   The other day I got a typewritten letter from Mr. Estell, and I sent it back to him without reading it.   Of course, he had to dictate it.   And he sent an apology by the next mail"

"Also dictated?" I asked.

"It would have been just like him," she laughed, "but it was scratched with a pen. I hate anything that's dictated; I actually hate it.   Some time ago I read that a favorite author of mine dictated his books or worked the typewriter himself, and since then I can't read him.   It seems to me that the mellowest work was done by the poets when they wrote with a quill.   Imagine Byron setting fire to a page with a typewriter!"

There was the humor of scorn in her "glad eyes" as she looked up at me.   "So, if I am to read your play, it must not be when the typewriter has hammered *you* out of it," she said.

"I will read it to you.   How will that do?"

"From the original sheets?   That will

do; that is, if you want to. I don't want you to feel that it's a duty."

"Oh, no; it will be a pleasure. The path of duty is too straight for me."

"It's the winding path that leads to the sweetest flowers," she said, with a motion of her hand toward a clump of roses not far away.

There were a hundred points on which I had yearned to question her, and the most vital of them all—why had she taken the name of that unsympathetic man?—arose to my mind, but instantly it sank again. Her manner toward me was cordial and intimate, but in it I recognized a command against familiarity; that quiet something which tells a man more than a volume of words could imply. I wanted to believe that she was persuaded by her father. I was willing to believe almost anything except that she could ever have loved him. It was not alone the eye of prejudice that made him look old; it was actual age. He was older than the Senator. But his people had been great—the lords of old Virginia. I would wait, and perhaps at some time in the future she might forget a high-strung woman's caution; she might drop a thoughtless word, a firefly to glow in the dark.

The negro preacher came walking slowly down the patch, to give his attention to another part of the garden. He was humming a tune, with his eyes on the ground, and he neither spoke nor halted, but at my feet he dropped a weed.

"You have a faithful gardener," I remarked, when Washington had passed beyond the reach of a low tone.

"Yes; there was only one George Washington, and there's only one Washington Smith."

"But don't you think he's a little too zealous?"

"Too zealous? How?" she inquired, turning her eyes full upon me.

"Well, I don't know that zealous is the word. Perhaps I should have said intolerant."

"Oh, he is intolerant—yes. He believes that he's one of the anointed."

"That's all very well, but he oughtn't to believe that he is appointed to look after the souls of other men."

"Then he would have no mission," she replied. "The true strength of the preacher is his sense of responsibility."

"Pardon me, I didn't know you were of the strictly orthodox fold."

"Didn't you? Don't you know I go to church every Sunday?"

"Yes, I ought to. I have more than once waited for you to come home." She looked at me in surprise, and I made haste to add: "The Senator and I have needed you to arbitrate our disputes, you know."

"Oh, yes, and I think you were wise in acknowledging that he had brought you into his party. We all take a great interest in our converts. Everybody is looking forward to the coming of your dramatic season," she went on after a moment's pause. "And I think you'll become quite a favorite

10

in society.   I heard Mrs. Atkinson speak of you. She's our leader.   She saw you somewhere. Of course there was some little prejudice against you, at first, but that has worn off.   And there's a splendid catch here for you—Miss Rodney—distantly related to the Estell family.   She has seen you, too.   She says you must be very romantic; and she asked me all sorts of questions."

"Of course I want to be agreeable, *but*—"

"But what?"

"I simply don't care anything for society."

"Our stupid society, you mean."

"No, I mean any society.   I like individuals but I don't care for sets."

"Oh, and you are going to rob me of the distinction of showing you off.   Very well, Sir."

"I wouldn't be a distinction—more of a humiliation."

"We'll see when the time comes.   You have no idea what a source of —what shall

I say? Pleasure — gratification you have been to me."

"Do you really mean it?"

"Mean it? Why shouldn't I? You have helped me to pick things to pieces; and we can have a great time when you know the people here well enough to gossip about them. It's always interesting to hear what a stranger has to say of one's old acquaintances."

"Yes, if he speaks what he conceives to be the truth. The truth is spicy and not infrequently malicious."

"You make me laugh. Do you suppose I want to hear anyone speak ill of my friends?"

"Why, yes. You might demur, but you would listen."

"Yes, I believe I would," she laughed, "and isn't it mean? I've tried so hard to be good, but I can't."

"It is hard to be good, and—" I hesitated.

"And what?"

"Will you pardon an impudence?"

"Yes, if it's not *too* bad."

"Hard to be good and beautiful."

Her face was turned from me, but I saw a red tint rise and spread over her neck. She spoke without looking at me, and her voice was steady and deep. "I helped you to set a trap and then walked into it, and therefore I've no right to feel offended, but if my treatment of you leads up to such compliments, I must change it."

"No!" I cried, abashed; and the negro on his knees at a tulip bed, down the path, looked up at me. "It was simply a jest; there has never been anything in your manner to warrant it. Let me tell you that at times I am a barbarian; I lose respect for polite customs. I have known ladies who liked to be told that they were beautiful—women who were charmed to have their pictures in a magazine among a collection of "types" celebrated for beauty. I—" was she laughing at me? She was.

"The fact that you take it so to heart

wipes out the impudence," she said, still laughing.

I felt that my crime existed in the fact that her husband was more than twenty year older than herself. And I have reason to believe that the young woman who marries an old man, and who is constantly striving to maintain her own self-respect, has a fancied or perhaps a real cause to stand in dread of a compliment. It may be sincere, but in its candor lies an insinuation and a reproach. But when Mrs. Estell saw that no insinuation was intended, she was even more free than she had been before. She laughed with such gayety that Washington went about his work and paid no further heed to us. We talked about the people of the town, the leader of society and the young woman who had been put forward as a splendid catch for me; and once I ventured near the verge of an awkward sentiment. In making a gesture she accidentally touched my hand, and with the thrill of the moment I could have leaped high in the air. But it took only a flash of reason to assure me that I was a fool. I will say, though, and without evil, that I would have given all my prospects, the theatre and the play—anything—to have clasped her in my arms. No, not anything. I would not have given up the respect which I hoped she had for me. Ah, how many hearts are this moment aching for a love that the law has hedged about with Duty! And this to me was monstrous, for I was of a mimic life, where love pretended that there were locksmiths to be laughed at, but where in reality the law itself was vain.

The Senator came striding down the path, and seeing me, he cried: "Ha! Mr. Manager, why didn't you have them wake me? Don't want to waste any more daylight than I am compelled to, but the fact is, I've been at work pretty hard of late. A campaign always stirs me up."

We made room for him and he sat down, continuing to talk. "Didn't hear about my speech out at Briar Flat last night, did you? Well, Sir, we had a lively time. You see the Convention is really the election, and to win I must get votes enough to secure the nomination. There's a Cheap John of a fellow announced as a candidate against anybody our party may put up, a schemer out after the country vote. Well, he came to our meeting—had no earthly business there, mind you, but he came. He interrupted me several times with his fool questions, and at last I said, 'See here, Mister Whatever - your - name - may- be, I am perfectly willing to answer any question that one of these farmers may ask, but I've got no time for a man who farms with his mouth.' Well, Sir, the boys laughed and he got red hot. He stood up and cried out that any man who said he wasn't a practical farmer and a gentleman was a liar. Huh! Well! I handed my hat to a friend and—"

"Now, father," Mrs. Estell broke in, "you promised me—"

"Hold on, now; it wasn't a fight. Nothing of the sort. I know what I promised you, and I'll keep my word. Yes, I handed my hat to a friend and stepped down to where the fellow stood, with his back against the wall. I asked him — I was polite—if he meant to insinuate that I was a liar. There was no violation of a promise in that, was there, Florence?"

"No, Sir, not if you asked him politely," she answered, laughing.

"It was polite, I assure you. Well, he studied a moment, and then declared that he never did insinuate, that he came right out and said what he meant. And, Belford, I rather admired him for that. But, er— the fact is—"

"You struck him," Mrs. Estell interjected. "Didn't you?"

"Well, that depends upon the way you look at it. Now, here, Florence, you wouldn't want to know that a man had stood up in front of a whole houseful of people and called your father a liar. I mean that under such circumstances you wouldn't blame me for—for tapping him."

"Of course not," she replied.

"Ah, ha, and I did tap him. Belford, I hit that fellow a crack that he'll remember the longest day he lives. Fell? Why, Sir, he fell like a beef; and when they had taken him away, the meeting was kind enough to name me as its unanimous choice."

The negro woman who had announced her suspicion of all men came out upon the veranda to ring the supper bell, and, astonished to realize that the sun was no longer shining, I bounced up with a declaration that I must get back to town.

"No, Sir, not till you have had supper," the Senator replied. "Why, what can you be thinking about to run away at a time like this? Come on," he added, taking my arm and turning me toward the house. "I want to have a talk with you after supper—on business. Come, Florence."

CHAPTER XII.

A MATTER OF BUSINESS.

IN the library, after supper, I waited for the Senator to introduce the talk which we were to have on business; but he wandered off into a political reminiscence of a day when a man found out what his convictions were and then looked about for a chance to defend them with his life. He told me, as comfortably he sat with his feet in the slippers which his daughter had brought for him, that he could recall an old fellow who wrote out his principles in blood drawn from his breast. ''Yes, Sir, and it created a big hurrah at the time. Copies of his creed were sought after, in the original ink, and so many of them were sent out that the suspicions of a young doctor were aroused. He calculated that the amount of blood thus put in outward circulation would leave an insufficient circulation within, though the body of the politician still appeared to be strong and active. And it was then that a most startling discovery was made. The rascal had not used his own blood, but a red powder and the juice of the pokeberry. Well, Sir, this stirred up the community from one end to the other; the people swore that they had been defrauded, and they demanded that he should make good the counterfeits or get out of the race. His circulating medium was not strong enough to warrant the output, so he retired in disgrace. Yes, Sir. Belford, do you know that I can see that fellow Petticord's hand every time I go to a political meeting? I can. He is all the time trying to tunnel under me, and it keeps me busy stepping about to keep from falling in. I am afraid, Sir, that sooner or later I'll have to kill that scoundrel."

"Father!" spoke his daughter, turning from the window.

"I beg your pardon, Florence. I don't mean to kill him—er—er—offensively, you understand, but, perhaps, necessarily. Of course we are inflicted more or less as we journey through this life, but I can't reconcile myself to the belief that we are called upon to stand everything. Let us say that sometimes the devil giveth and the Lord taketh away. Now, if I could only provoke him into a fight—I beg your pardon."

Mrs. Estell had put her hand on his shoulder. She looked at me with a smile, but the Senator glanced up to meet an expression of reproof.

"Provoke him into a fight?" she said.

"Figuratively, you understand. I wouldn't provoke him except figuratively. But I don't see why my footsteps are to be constantly dogged by that red wolf. Why doesn't he come out in his paper and give me a chance? What are you going to do?" She had stepped upon a chair and was taking down the foils. "Belford, I reckon you'll have to defend yourself. I won't fight; I'm a noncombatant."

I fenced with her, having had some little experience, but she was too quick and too skillful for me. The Senator laughed, and his face was aglow with pride to see her drive me into a corner, where I was willing enough to surrender.

"He isn't strong enough yet," she said, in excuse of my defeat.

"Oh, yes, he is," the Senator cried. "He's as strong as a deck hand, but he hasn't the skill. Just feel of that girl's arm, Belford. Don't be afraid of her—she won't hurt you."

I put my hand on her arm, so round and firm, so warm through the gauze sleeve she wore; and I thought it well for me that neither the father nor the daughter observed my agitation.

A negro came to tell the Senator that a Mr. Spencer wanted to speak to him at the gate. "Politics," said the law maker, as he took up his hat. "And that fellow wouldn't get off his horse to meet the President. Stay right where you are till I come back, Belford. I want to have a talk with you—on business."

He went out and Mrs. Estell sat down in his armchair. Her face was flushed and her eyes were a delight to behold.

"I'll be glad when this miserable campaign is over," she said. "It upsets everything, spoils our evenings, and bores everybody that comes to the house."

"It doesn't bore me," I replied.

"No; I gave him his orders not to talk politics to you."

"That's a compliment, surely."

"Oh, I don't know. I told him he ought to see that you didn't understand the political situation. And after he'd converted you he was willing enough to grant you freedom. Mr. Belford, why haven't you told me more about yourself?"

And this gave me the opportunity to ask her why she had not told me more about herself, her days of romance.

"I have had no such days," she said. "I was born here and I live here and that is all. But you have been everywhere; you came from an old and poetic country."

"And you," I replied, "have always lived in a poetic country."

"No, dreamy and visionary, but hardly poetic. Poetry means action and adventure. You have never told me about *her?*"

"Her? What her do you mean?"

"Oh, any her. There must have been one."

"No; I can't recall one."

"Really? And you so sentimental?"

"I'm not sentimental. A sentimentalist would tint the truth while I would rather view it in its natural color, be it dun or even black. Do you believe we ought to be held responsible for everything?"

"Yes, nearly everything."

"But suppose a man forgets to lock the door of his heart, and a woman out in the dark, feeling about, accidentally lifts up the latch and comes in. She is pure and innocent and she does not know that she is warming herself at the hearth of a heart. Ought he to put her out and shut the door?"

"No, he should make the fire still warmer and brighter, if she has come out of the cold and the dark."

"But suppose her lawful place is beside another fire?"

"Then she would not stray from it."

"But say that she is walking in her sleep?"

"She would run away as soon as she awakes."

"Ah, but suppose she does not awake. Should he put her out?"

"I—I don't know. He must not leave his door unlocked—he should—should even bar his windows."

We heard the Senator coming down the hallway and were silent. "Now what do you reckon that fool fellow wanted? Well, Sir, it beats anything. Told me that he had named a boy for me—said that it ought to be worth five dollars and a barrel of flour.

Why, dog my cats—beg your pardon (bowing to Mrs. Estell). But I say, if it were to get out—no, keep your seat, I'll sit over here—get out that I am giving five dollars and a barrel of flour for each boy named for me, why, I'd be broke in six months. A long time ago a yellow-looking chap from the swamps came to tell me that he had given my name to as fine a boy as the country ever saw. I was a little easier flattered in those days than I am now, and it tickled me mightily; and what did I do but give the fellow a twenty-dollar gold piece. Well, Sir, about six months after that he went to a friend of mine, a candidate to fill an unexpired term of county clerk, and declared that he had just named a splendid specimen of a boy for him. And now what do you suppose we found out? The villain changed that boy's name every time a campaign came along. Yes, Sir, and he was about ten years old when he was given my name."

"By the way, there was something you wanted talk to me about," I said, to remind him that the hour was growing late. "Something on business, I understood you to say."

"Yes, but there's plenty of time. Let me see, now, what it was I had on my mind. Something I wanted to say about—well, Sir, it has escaped me."

"Then it couldn't have been very important," said Mrs. Estell.

"It couldn't, eh? Now that's where you are wrong. In this life we are prone to forget the most important things. My old grandfather used to forget his wife when she went visiting with him, and go on home without her. But come to consider more closely, it wasn't exactly a business matter I wanted to talk to you about, Belford. I wanted to tell you that day after to-morrow we'll go fox-hunting. I sent over to the plantation to have the hounds put in good condition, and they'll be ready for us. Ever ride after the hounds?"

"Only in a mimic chase—a bag of anis-seed."

"Oh, what nonsense! Do you know

what ought to be done with a man that would get up such a disgrace on the greatest of all sport? Ought to be deprived of his citizenship, his vote; and I don't know of anything much worse than that. Now, you be here day after to-morrow morning, and I'll show you what it is to live like a white man."

He was so earnest and so set in his conviction that no work, however important, should be permitted to stand as a stumbling-block in the road leading to the field of this essential sport, that I yielded, but reluctantly, until Mrs. Estell dropped a word of persuasion, and then I could not have found the moral nerve to urge even the most courteous objection.

When I took my leave, soon afterward, the Senator walked out with me, through the gate and down the road; and when he halted to turn back, I looked round and saw Mrs. Estell standing on the portico, with a lamp held aloft to light his way.

CHAPTER XIII.

THE PLACE OF THE GOBLINS.

DOWN the road not far from Talcom's house there stood a stone chimney, tall and white, in the midst of a dark thicket of scrub locust, the mark of a fire that years ago had burnt a miser and melted his gold. It was a desolate place, even in the sunlight, for the air that breathed an enchantment in the Senator's magnolia garden came hither to whine and moan. And whenever at night I passed this place I was chilled with a nervous fear that a goblin might jump out and grab me. I knew that there were no goblins, in the sun, but the night is the mother of many an imp that the day refuses to father.

I walked slower as I came abreast of the

thicket, to prove to myself that I was not afraid, yet ready to take to my heels, when suddenly I halted, statue-still, with a gasp and a loud beating of the heart. A great black figure plunged out of the bushes, into the road, and in another moment I am sure that I should have run like a deer had not a voice familiar to my ear exclaimed:

"Fo' de Lawd, I didn' know I wuz comin' through dat place. Walkin' 'cross de pasture thinkin', an' de fust thing I knowed—"

"That you, Washington?" I cried.

"Yes, Sir. Oh, it's Mr. Belford," he said, coming forward.

"You almost scared the life out of me."

"Yes, Sir, and scared myself, too. I am on my way from prayer meeting, and my mind was so occupied that I didn't think of the thicket until I was into it. Going to town? I'll walk a piece with you if you have no objections."

"None at all; be glad to have you. It made you forget your education," said I, as we walked along.

"It did that, Sir. It makes no difference how many colleges a colored man has gone through nor how many books he has read, scare him and he is what the white people call a nigger. My mother used to tell me stories about that place back there, and I can't forget them. But Miss Florence isn't afraid of it, Sir. When a child she often played there alone, after dark, and the Senator would have to go after her. Pardon me, but why did you cry 'No!' so loud in the garden!"

"Why, it must have been when I was reciting something."

He grunted and we strode on in silence until he said: "Mr. Belford, I have heard that there is no moral responsibility among the people that play on the stage—that the winning or losing of love means little to them. Is it true?"

"Washington, I have read of a hundred scandals in the church. Were they true?"

He did not answer at once; he strode for a long time in silence, and then he spoke:

"There are bad people everywhere, and some of them carry the outward form of the cross, but it is made of light paper and not of heavy wood. But there are many who carry the true cross. Let us, however, put that aside, for I must turn back when we get to the first gaslight down yonder, and there is something I want to say to you if I can get at it properly."

"Out with it; don't try to lead up to it."

"You are in love with Mrs. Estell," he bluntly said, and I had expected something to the point, but nothing so straightforward and undiplomatic; and I could have knocked him down for his impertinence, but I swallowed my wrath and waited for him to proceed.

"I can see it."

"But can she?" I compelled myself, quietly, to ask.

"No. If she were to see it, she would never step into your presence again."

"But the Senator! Can he see it?"

"No. Honor makes him blind to such a

sight. He could not understand such a violation of hospitality. He has made you
almost a member of his family; your misfortune demanded his sympathy, and he
gave you his confidence."

"Then you stand alone with your eyes
open?" I replied.

"I may stand alone, but other eyes are
open—and they wink at one another."

"What! Do you mean that the neighbors—"

"Yes," he broke in, "that is what I
mean—the neighbors."

"Washington, you were graduated from
the Fisk University, I understand, an insti-
tution made possible by the generosity of a
band of jubilee singers; and, having been
educated at the instance of song, I should
think that you would have aspired to poesy
rather than to stilted talk and a detective's
disposition to pry into affairs that don't
concern you."

With the slouching habit of his race, he
had been dragging his feet along, but now

his heels struck hard upon the road. He sighed like a steam valve, to lessen the pressure of his boiling resentment, but he did not speak. I expected him to turn back in silence, as we were now beneath the light of the street lamp, but he did not; he strode forward as if vaguely in quest of some sort of support, and put his hand on the lamp-post, a hand so black that it looked like a bulge of the iron. And then he turned to me. "Mr. Belford," he said, "an educated negro is an insult to every unthinking white man. And unless he jabbers they call him stilted. Let me tell you, Sir, that I have stretched myself on the floor to read by the firelight because I couldn't afford to buy a candle—struggling to conquer the dialect of my father—and now you reproach me with it. My poor and ignorant people wouldn't listen to me if I talked as they do. Heaven, to them, is a place of magnificence, and the man who paints the picture of Paradise for them must use extravagant colors. Sir, I am no more stilted than you are; you serve the devil on stilts."

I had to laugh, and then I apologized. "There is a good deal of truth in what you say," said I. "The actor struts, and just as you do, to impress the unthinking. But let us drop it. I'm sorry I offended you. But, really, I don't like your interference."

"It is not an interference. I am an old servant of that family. Look here!" He snatched his hand from the lamp-post and folded his arms. "What do you intend shall be the outcome?"

"I don't know—I don't see—"

"Don't see the end," he interposed. "But don't you think that the end of everything ought to be kept well in view?"

"Yes, I do. But sometimes a beginning is so delightful that we are afraid to look toward the end. But I realize my own selfishness, and I acknowledge to you that in spite of what you may term the immoral atmosphere of a player's life—I confess, or, rather, I affirm, that in my blood there is a strong current of good old English puritanism; and I will swear to you that I would cut my own throat rather than to bring disgrace upon that family."

He put his mighty hands upon my shoulders, and, turning my face to the light, he looked hard into my eyes.

"No man could say more, Mr. Belford. But what are you going to do?"

"I am going to stay away from—from her."

"When, Mr. Belford; when will you begin to stay away?"

"I have promised to go fox-hunting day after to-morrow."

"And after that?"

"I will not go to the house."

He took my hand, and I forgot that he was a stilted and officious negro. "Good night, Mr. Belford." He turned away, but faced about and said: "I am going to a cabin on the hillside — to pray for you. Good-night."

CHAPTER XIV.

OLD JOE VARK.

THE town was going to bed; the late moon was rising. and in the mag-nolia gardens there seemed to waver a bright and shadowy silence—a night when every sound was afar off, a half mysterious echo—the closing of a window shutter, the subdued footfall of a thief, the indistinct notes of an old song lagging in the soft and lazy air. I walked about the courthouse, its pillars classic in the shadow, its gilded cupola gaudy in the light. I did not turn to my habitation across the square, to sniff the lifeless atmosphere and the sick-ish paint of the opera house; I bent my way to the river where the moon was free. And upon a rotting yawl I sat down to think, shoulder to shoulder with the ghost of a dead commerce. Far across the stream a mud scow fretted and fluttered like a duck in distress, making just enough of noise to cry "silence" in the ear of night.

There is religion in the reverie of even an atheist; and in the meditation of a free-thinker, whose grandfather was a believer, there is almost a confession of faith. I thought of all that the negro had said; I reviewed his earnestness and saw his look of trouble; I pictured Talcom in his trust-fulness; I saw his daughter in her unsuspecting innocence, impulsive, almost eccentric, and yet a type of the South. I thought of it all, and I swore that I would keep faith with the preacher. I swore it with my hand held up, I ground myself down until I felt the rotting old boat crumbling beneath me, and yet it seemed that some devil arose in the air maliciously to whisper, "No you won't." And in this reproach, intended to tantalize the conscience, there was a shameful sweetness, a promise that again I should sit in the garden with her. But I went to bed strong, and I arose with strength the next morning. I would chase a fox with her, and then, I should see her no more, except by accident.

The Senator had enjoined me not to appear overglad to make acquaintances; not to invite the approach of the idle, lest they should become familiar, but it was hard to maintain dignity in the presence of such good humor and friendliness. A man whom I might have passed a hundred times, without suspecting his importance, would stop me to say that his name was Hopgood or Leatherington or Yancey; to assure me that his grandfather, after having come out of the Mexican War, had served as Clerk of the Circuit Court; that he was pleased to welcome me to Bolanyo; that it was about his time of day (looking at his watch) to take a drink, and that he would be pleased to have me join him. I had not the nerve nor the dignity to cool these warm advances, rich in a yellowing sort of humor, the sad fun of a dying importance; and I found that the Senator, himself, while pretending to preserve the austerity of a high position, brought matters close to earth by putting his arm about some old fellow to laugh over an ancient and shady joke. In the town there was one man who scouted the idea of self-importance, except when drunk, and then he sometimes assumed to own the community. This man was Joe Vark, a shoe-maker.

In the forenoon, the day after my moral vow had been taken, I went into his shop. He was sitting on his low bench; and he looked up, with a number of shoe-pegs showing between his lips, and mumbled me an invitation to sit down. He was short, with a fine head and thin, light hair. His wrinkled face was rather pale and clean of beard. Beside him lay a book, held partly open by an old shoe sole.

"Well, how are they coming?" he inquired, talking through his teeth.

"All right," I answered, and he looked up with a twinkle in his eye. I waited for him to say something, but he went on with his work, taking a peg from his lips and driving it into a shoe.

"You were not born here, were you, Mr. Vark?"

He drove five or six pegs, until there were no more between his lips, loosened the strap with which he held the shoe upon a piece of iron, whistled softly as he examined his work, looked up at me and said:

"No, I came here from Pennsylvania a long time ago. And it was years before they granted me the privilege of being natural when I was drunk. Oh, it was all right to get drunk, mind you, but they wanted me to be quiet; and I hold that a man who acts about the same, drunk or sober, is dangerous to a community. Oh, they meet you with a warm shake, but it takes years to become one of them. But after you do get to be one of them you are proud of it. Yes, Sir, and about all I've got to boast of is that I've been here more than thirty years. I'm not worth a cent, you understand, but I'm as proud as a peacock. What of? That I've lived here thirty years. What of it? Everything of it. I can take a few drinks and be natural. Not long ago I had a little row and I snatched a comparative stranger from one side of the street to the other. And what did they do with me? Why, I had been here so long that the judge couldn't do anything. He fined the other fellow for being a stranger and that settled it."

He put more pegs between his lips, adjusted the shoe on the iron and resumed his work. The shop was small and dingy, and the floor, almost hidden by scraps of leather, had doubtless never been swept. An encased stairway from the outside made a low, dark corner, and here, on a shelf, the old man kept an array of books. It was said that he sometimes indulged in a reading spree, just after a season of liquor; and then he slammed his door in the face of the

present and lived locked up with the long
ago.

I did not disturb him, but waited for his
spirit to move of its own accord. He
pegged the shoe, removed the strap, and
from a small bottle that hung on the wall
within reach he blackened the edge of the
sole; he inserted a hook, pulled out the
last, and set the shoe aside to dry. Then
he took up an old boot and said: "This
thing is beyond all repair. Ought to have
been thrown away years ago. But the fool
would leave it here, and I'm expecting him
every minute. Heigho, I don't know what
to do with it. Guess I'll put it aside until
he comes, and then beg him to take it down
and throw it into the river."

He threw the boot aside, took up a piece
of leather and began to examine it. Then,
brushing everything aside, he picked up a
clay pipe, and as he was filling it, I handed
him a lighted match.

"Thank you." He lighted his pipe,
puffing it with a loud smack of the lips, and

then settled himself down to talk. "No use of a man killing himself with work. I've been here too long for that. How are you and Talcom getting along?"

"First rate. I have never met a more genial companion—never bores, always interesting."

"Yes, Talcom is a good fellow. He'll recommend a gold brick, and then, to prove his sincerity, he'll turn round and buy it himself. He held me off for a long time. Of course I never expected him to make a brother of me—our lines keep us too far apart for that—but he's friendly, and has done me many a favor. But I lived here a long time under suspicion, and whenever anything was stolen they naturally looked to me. But, gradually, I convinced them that I was inclined to be honest."

"By going to church?" I inquired.

"Oh, no, by accepting a challenge from a rival shoemaker to fight a duel. The fellow backed down; his custom came to me, and he went away. I am under great obligations to that man—best friend I ever had; don't know what would have become of me if he hadn't backed out."

"But you would have fought him."

"Well, I don't know about that. I do know, however, that I felt like hugging him when he refused to fight. Yes," he went on, after a short pause and an industrious puffing at his pipe, "Talcom is all right. But you never can tell which way he'll jump in his likes and dislikes. He may like a man and he may not, and he's as sudden as a gun going off. You caught him—not by anything you could have said or done, but you just happened to fit him."

"All hands at home?" came a voice as whining as a mendicant's plea, and, looking up, I recognized the gaunt and drooping form of the notorious Bugg Peters. He stood for a moment in the doorway, and then came forward with a slouching lurch, with a grin and nod at me and a bow of profound respect for the "boss" of the shop.

"Look here, Bugg," said the shoemaker, "I can't do anything with that old boot. It's beyond all repair.   Take it out somewhere and throw it away."

"Fur mercy sake, Joe, don't talk like that," protested the notorious one, dropping upon a bench and humping over as if his upper muscles had given away.   "Don't snatch all the hope right out of a feller's hand.   That boot belongs to my youngest son-in-law, and unless he gets it mended to-day he can't come to town to-morrow. Joe, you've just got to fix it.   Say, got about as fine a chunk of a boy down at my house as you ever see'd in your life.   Nan's."

"Nan's?   How many does that make?" the shoemaker asked.

"Let me see.   Why, it makes somewhere in the neighborhood of six for Nan. And her old man is settin' right there by the fireplace now a-shakin' fitten to kill himself.   He ain't no account at all except in the fall of the year, and then I take him out in the woods and let him shake down

persimmons.   Mister (speaking to me), they
tell me you are goin' to start a show here,
and I'll fetch my folks to see it if I can
raise a few chickens and sell 'em.   Thought
I'd get some aigs to-day.   Got three old
hens and I thought I'd put 'em to work.
But, look here, Joe, you ain't in earnest
about not bein' able to do nothin' with that
boot?"

"Yes, I am, Bugg.   Throw it away."

"Now, when did you expect a man to
get so rich as to fling away his property?
Doesn't the Scripture say, 'Waste not, for
to-morrow you may die?'   Grab a-hold of
her, Joe, and patch her up.   All you've got
to do is to put leather where there ain't
none."

"Yes, all I've got to do is to build a boot
in the air."

"Well, but ain't that your business, hah?"

"Yes, if I'm paid for it; but you haven't
paid for the last pair of shoes I half-soled.
And you said you'd pay on the following
Wednesday."

"Did I say that? But I didn't tell you pointedly. You can always count on me when I tell you pointedly. A man that won't pay when he tells you pointedly is a liar. Whose boots are them right there—them old ones? They'd just about fit my son-in-law. Yes, Sir; and he can put 'em on and come up to town and enjoy himself. What will you take for 'em, Joe?"

"Two dollars, Bugg."

"Cheap enough, and I'll take 'em. Pass 'em over."

"But when will you pay for them?"

"Let me see. I'll pay for 'em Thursday."

"Pointedly?" the shoemaker inquired, with a wink at me.

"Well, now, if it's to be pointedly I'd better make it Thursday week. How does that hit you?"

"Take them along, but I'll never get the money."

He tumbled forward from his seat, grabbed up the boots, and, holding them close to his bosom, he said:

" Joe, don't—don't insult me by sayin' that you'll never get your money. It's a sad thing to give your word pointedly and I've give you mine."

He took out a string, tied the boots together at the straps and threw them across his shoulder. Then he sat down. "Yes, Sir," he said, "when a man gives me his word pointedly and fails to keep it, I put him down in my liar book. Say, Mister, I hear 'em say you are goin' to give your show in a house. Don't see how you can give much of a show unless you've got room to gallop around in, but I reckon you'll do the best you can. Joe, let me take a few of them books along with me, " he added, nodding toward the shelf. And the shoemaker's hand, with a movement as quick as the frisk of a squirrel's tail, flew upon the bench at his side and rattled the tools, as if grabbing for a hammer to throw at the head of the outrageous customer. His face was hard and his eyes were set with anger, and if for a moment there was not murder in his heart, he gave me a bit of fine acting. But his epileptic resentment passed away with a jerk, and looking up at the dumfounded Peters, he said, "Bugg, I guess you'd better go."

"Why, what's the matter, Joe?"

"Guess you'd better go. I can stand to be robbed of leather, but when you try to extend your theft to the things that make me superior to you ignorant yaps, I feel like mashing your head."

"Your driftwood is comin' so swift that I can't ketch it, Joe."

"He means that you must not touch his books," I put in.

"Oh, that's all right," Peters replied. "I'm not hankerin' after 'em. Just thought I'd take a few of 'em along to get 'em out of the way. Joe, if you happen down in my range drap in and see Nan's boy. Tickle you mighty nigh to death."

He slouched away, and the shoemaker resumed his work. I had been sitting there in a strong draught of the town's atmos-

phere, with two characters for my play; and,
taking my leave, I felt that I hugged a
greater possession than Peters had found
when he tied the boots together and threw
them across his shoulder.

CHAPTER XV.

OLD AUNT PATSEY.

LIKE a boy in his yearning to have Santa Claus come, I went early to bed to force the dawning of another day. I resorted to the tricks that men have employed to induce drowsiness; I counted sheep bounding over a fence, a hundred, a thousand, until their number exceeded the Patriarch's fold, and yet I lay there wide awake, with my nerves starting at every noise, before it reached my ears. I strove to trace the filmy thread that lies between consciousness and sleep, and I fancied that it was a raveling from a rainbow, with one end in the sunset, the other in the sunrise. I reached a place where the thread was broken and now the world was dark, but, feeling about, I found the two ends of the silken line, and put them together, and when they touched, the world flashed up in a blaze of light—the sun was shining.

No exact hour had been fixed for the meet at the Senator's house, and I was beset by the fear that a desire not to be early might make me late. Common sense dictated a middle resort, but in my nervous anxiety I had no common sense. Why so sensitive and timorous now when I had been so bold a few days before? I had promised the negro preacher and myself that this day should see the end of a relationship.

I set out earlier than the time I had fixed, expecting to loiter along the road, to breathe sweet air beneath the roses that hung above the old garden walls; but, giving no heed to the roses, I passed them hurriedly, as a hasty reader skips a beautiful sentence in eagerness to snatch the excitement of a closing scene. I passed the lamp-post and thought of the negro's black hand, a knot on the iron; I came abreast of the old chimney and the thicket, the lair of the goblins at night.

And here I halted to gaze at the Senator's house, the pillared portico, the cool yard, the martin box on a tall pole, the magnolia garden. And now my progress toward the gate was slow, with the minute and sense- less observation of little things; a bit of sheep's wool on a brier bush; an old shoe half buried in the sandy drain beside the road; the heavy gate-latch, made by a clumsy blacksmith; the uneven bricks in the short walk between the gate and the portico; a stone and a shell on the step, where someone had cracked a nut.

I was admitted by the negress whose motto was "suspicion." She gave me a broad grin and nodded toward the parlor; and I heard strange voices and laughter. Just as I reached the door, Mrs. Estell stepped out into the hall. A magnolia bloom fell from her hand, and she laughed as she stooped to pick it up, and when she looked at me her face was red, though not with embarrassment, but with stooping, for she spoke and her voice was deep and clear and her eyes were not abashed.

"Oh, you are just in time, Mr. Belford. I want you to meet some friends of mine, and my aunt is here, too. I know you'll like her, she's so queer."

I would have staid to ask her why she supposed me to be attracted by queer persons, but she touched my arm, and as an automaton I turned toward the parlor and stepped into the room, to meet Mr. Elkin, a frail and timid-looking young fellow with plastered hair; Miss Rodney, a pinkish creature of uncertain age, the "splendid catch" which Mrs. Estell had set aside for me; and Mrs. Braxon, the aunt. She looked queer, and I could not have denied that she interested me. She was very tall, straight and stiff, with eyes that suggested a savage. Into her aged mouth the artifice of the dentist had put the teeth of youth, and, not yet accustomed to them, she imposed upon her lips the double exertion of talking with her jaws shut.

"Well," she said, looking hard at me, "and you are the man that Giles has been telling me so much about? But, conscience alive, he ought to have something to talk of besides politics."

"You are his favorite sister, I believe," I replied, with the giggle of Miss Rodney in my ears.

"Do you? Well, I married his brother, if that's what you mean."

"Is he living?" I inquired.

"Florence," she said, "it's strange that you haven't told Mr. What's-his-name anything about me. Every time I come here I come as a stranger, a rank stranger."

"Why, Aunt Patsey, I told him—"

"She told me a great deal about you, Mrs. Braxon," I put in, "but my memory is, you might say, not good."

"Oh, yes, and I suppose Giles Talcom told you all about me, too; told you that I was his favorite sister, didn't he? Well, it's all right. Miss Rodney, what *are* you giggling about?"

"Why, nothing at all, Mrs. Braxon," the young woman declared, growing pinker. The old lady looked at Elkin, and he started and slammed his knees together. I glanced at Mrs. Estell, and she hid her eyes from me, afraid to laugh.

"Where do you live?" I inquired of the old lady.

"Up in the Tennessee hills, and every time I come down in this low ground I want to get back. The laziest folks I ever saw in my life, and the niggers ain't worth their salt. And the way Giles pets that black preacher makes me sick, a-buying of his church bells to keep folks awake at night. I'd make him chop down them good-for-nothing trees out there and plant onions. That's what I'd do with him. Florence, where did Giles go?"

"Why, he sent word over to the plantation to have his hounds brought last night, but, somehow, the message wasn't delivered, and so he has gone after them himself. We want to start from here—"

"After the hounds?   Start where?"

"Fox-hunting."

The old woman cleared her throat with an ach, ach.   "Fox-hunting?   Is it possible that he keeps up that foolishness? Chasing a fox, when there's so much to be done in this world?   I read in a paper yesterday that a woman had starved to death in New Orleans, and here you all are, going to chase a fox."

"Why, Mrs. Braxon," the young man spoke up, "we can't help that.   If we let the fox go it won't bring the woman back to life."

She looked at him and his knees flew together.   "But you could be raising something for folks to eat."

"Yes, ma'am, but we raise more now than we can sell."

She looked at him with a bow and a smirk of contempt.   "More than you can sell.   Yes, of course.   More than you can sell to a woman that's starving.   Yes, of course."

13

"But nobody starves to death in Bolanyo, Aunt Patsey," Mrs. Estell remarked.
"We take care of our poor; and it was a
mere accident that the woman starved in
New Orleans."

"Oh, you do? A mere accident. Of
course. Are you going to chase a fox?"
the old woman asked, with her eyes on
Miss Rodney.

"I have been invited to go, and—"

"Of course. But, go on, and don't let
anything I say prevent you. I staid at
home, year in and year out, and never went
anywhere, while my husband was a-gal-
loping over the country, a-blowing of his
horn and a-chasing of foxes; and folks in a
town not more than twenty miles away
were as hungry as they could be. But,
after he died, I didn't stay at home, I tell
you. I went out and looked for hungry
folks, and I fed 'em, too. Talk to me
about chasing a fox."

"Auntie," said Mrs. Estell, smiling upon
the old lady, indeed, approaching her and

bending with graceful tenderness over her chair, "you try to make people believe that you are hard to get along with, but you are the sweetest thing. She snaps and snarls to hide the tenderness of her heart, Mr. Belford."

"I do nothing of the sort. For goodness' sake, child, take your hands off me. Stop fussing with me. Go over there and sit down. A body would think that I'm so old that you are standing here ready to catch me when I start to fall over. Go along with you!"

Mrs. Estell, laughing, pressed her radiant cheek against the widow's whitening hair. "I like to have half tearful fun with you, Aunt Patsey," she said.

"Oh, you do. Well, get away and don't pretend that you think anything of me. I have no money to leave you."

Elkin laughed. The old woman looked at him and he clapped his knees together. "I—I—beg your pardon," he stammered.

"She's so delightful," said Miss Rodney,

leaning toward me.   "Quite a character for
the stage, papa says.   And when does your
house open?"

"Not before October," I answered.

"And not until he can get a good company," said Mrs. Estell, standing in front of
us.   " I have enough interest in the house to
demand that much.   Oh, there comes father
with the hounds and I'm not ready yet."

She ran away, and though the sun was
in the window, the room was darker now,
and a shadow seemed to lie where she had
stood.   We heard the Senator's horn and
the impatient cry of the hounds.

" I'd rather hunt a bear than a fox," said
the young man.   "I went with a party of
fellows down in the canebrake last fall and
a bear killed four dogs.   Just grabbed 'em
up like this (hugging himself) and crushed
'em.   Just broke their bones.   Just grabbed
'em up this way and mashed 'em.   Didn't
look like it was any trouble at all.   Just—
just squeezed the life out of 'em.   I had—
I had a dog named Ring — great big dog—

and he grabbed him up this way, the bear did, and old Ring just gave one howl and that was the end of it.   Bear didn't appear to mind it.   Just seemed like he was enjoying himself, but we hadn't agreed to keep him in all the dogs he wanted to kill, so we shot him."

"You did?" said the old lady, smirking at him.   "Do tell.   And you'd rather stand there and see him kill those poor dogs than to chase a fox."

"Oh, I—I don't mean that I like to see the dogs killed, Mrs. Braxon, I mean I—"

"Would rather see a bear with his arms full of poor dogs than to chase a fox.   Yes, I know what you mean."

In came the Senator.   He bowed to the ladies, cried "Ha!" to the young man and seized my hand as if a year had elapsed since we parted.   "Belford, I've got a horse for you that can clear any fence in the State."

"With me on his back?" I asked.

"Yes, I hope so.   You can try, you know, and if you can't keep your seat why you must fall as easily as you can. Sister Patsey, you look as bright as a dollar."

"Go on with your blarney, Giles. I've got no dollar to leave to you."

"And bless your life, I'm glad of it. But it's time we were going. Where's Florence?"

"Gone to get ready for your nonsense," Mrs. Braxon answered. "Oh, you men! Not half of you are worth your salt."

"No," said the Senator. "And if there comes a time when men are worth their salt and women are worth their pepper, humanity will be well seasoned, eh, Belford? But we must be making a move. Elkin, help Miss Rodney to mount, please."

"Yes, and I guess I've got to buckle my girth tighter," said the young man. "Come, Miss Minnie, and let me help you up."

Just as they passed out there came a slow step down the hall. "Why, it's Estell!" cried the Senator. "Why, hello, Tom, we didn't expect you for a week. And, Sir, here's your Aunt Patsey."

Estell was carrying a cane in his right

hand and he stuck out one finger for me to shake. But when in the same manner he presumed to greet the old lady, she stormed at him: "Look here, Tom Estell, don't give me no one finger to shake. Andrew Jackson gave me his whole hand when I was a child, and I want no one finger now. That's like it," she added, as he put his cane under his arm and gave her his hand.

Mrs. Estell entered the room. "Why, you old surprise party," she cried. He stepped forward, but, catching sight of her riding habit, he halted.

"What does all this mean?" he asked.

"Why, we were going fox-hunting, dear."

"You—you going?"

"Why, yes. You have never objected."

"But I do now."

"Very well," she replied, beginning to pull at her gloves.

"Tom," cried the Senator, "what the devil—I mean the deuce—is the matter with you?"

And then Aunt Patsey broke out, jump-

ing from her chair and shaking her finger at Estell: "You are trying to smother
the God-given spirit of that child, and you
ought to be ashamed of yourself. You hate
to see her run—you want to see her dodder
about like an old man. What earthly harm
can there be in her going fox-hunting? Better men than you ever dared be have chased
foxes and have let their wives go, too.
Don't you dare say a word to me—don't
you dare!"

Estell turned about and strode with sullen
step to the foot of the stairs, the Senator
passing him without saying a word. I was
standing at the door, and I stepped aside to
let Mrs. Estell pass, but she lingered in the
parlor, as if to speak to her aunt, as if, in
truth, she would put her arms about the
old woman's neck; and I turned my back,
to face the State Treasurer, standing at the
foot of the stairs. Our eyes met, but he
was silent, and I had nothing to say. Mrs.
Estell came out into the hall, but returned
almost instantly to the old woman, and

Estell trod wearily to the upper floor. His wife came out, and she looked up with duty's self-conscious smile.

"May I speak a word?" I asked. "Just one?"

"Two," she answered.

"I promised to read my play to you."

"Yes; and you will—"

"Not keep my promise."

We were walking slowly toward the stairway, she slightly in advance. But now her feet were quick, until she reached the stair, and then she halted, turned to me, and said:

"Mr. Belford, any man can make a promise, but sometimes it requires a *gentleman* to break one."

I had no reply to make; I was the interloper. I bowed to her, and, snatching my hat from the halltree, I passed out upon the portico.

"Yes, I am mighty sorry," the Senator was saying to Elkin and Miss Rodney, who sat upon their horses at the gate—"sorry as I ever was in my life, but my horse stuck a nail in his foot and can hardly walk. Of course I could get another horse, but take Felix out of the chase and the whole thing falls flat. And my best hound is sick, too. Sometimes it does seem that everything stands in the way. But we'll have it, now, very soon. Get down, and stay to dinner. Ah, Belford, you going? Well, I'll see you in a day or two."

CHAPTER XVI.

THE PLAY.

I DREADED the embarrassment of meeting the Senator again; and it was with a sense of nervousness that I looked from my office window, the next morning, to see him getting out of his buggy. He came briskly up the stairs, spoke heartily to someone whom he met on the landing, halted at my open door, and, hat in hand, made me a sweeping bow.

"Ha, early to work is the thing," he said, stepping into the room and glancing about. "More pictures of famous players, I see. Well, we'll have them strutting about our stage the first thing they know. How do you feel?" he asked, drawing up a chair and sitting down.

"First rate—too well, I might say. This air makes me content to sit and dream."

"Good; it is better to find contentment even in a dream than to snap our nerves in two with chasing what we might regard substantial happiness. Why, confound it all, Belford, there is no such thing as substantial happiness. Anything substantial is too material, too gross; and happiness is a certain spiritual condition of the mind. Therefore, I say, let the old South dream if she feels like it. There used to be an old fellow that lived about here—Mose Parish. Well, the time came for Mose to die; but he wasn't scared, not a bit of it. A preacher came to talk to him, and old Mose listened for a while, and then he said: 'Oh, no, I never did much of anything—never built a steamboat nor a house, but I've had a good deal of fun, and I hold that when a man is having fun he can't have it all alone; he's helping some other fellow.'"

We talked about hundreds of things, and touched occasionally upon our business venture, but nothing led to a subject which I felt, and which he seemed to feel, was too delicate to be mentioned. He gossiped of young Elkin's affection for Miss Rodney; he said that Elkin's love put him in mind of an ass with gilded ears. He spoke of the coming election and the surety with which he and Tom Estell would win; but when he took his leave he did not invite me to call at the house. I met him day after day, in the office, in the street, in the rotunda of the hotel; and he always greeted me with a warm and earnest cordiality, but at parting he would say, " I'll see you again soon;" and never that I should come to see him.

I walked a great deal, musing over my play, and more than once in rebellion my feet wandered from their usual path to tread the sacred and forbidden ground that lay in the neighborhood of the Senator's home. Near the close of day, I sometimes saw him sitting on the portico, with his chair tipped back, his feet against a classic pillar, smoking his pipe—a vandalic American indulging a national posture to the shame of a Grecian memory.   Once I saw his daughter standing near him, where the fading sunlight fell, gazing afar off, shading her eyes with her hand.   And she might have seen me had I not bent behind a bush; had I been less a thief.

One hot afternoon the Senator came into the office, fanning himself with his hat.

"No dreaming now, Belford," said he. "It's too hot even to doze.   What's all that you've got spread out there?"

"Our play," I answered.

"Oh, yes.   And, by George, there seems to be enough of it.   Let me hear a chapter or two.   Isn't in chapters, though, is it? Fire away and let me hear what it sounds like.   You look like a commissioner of deeds, with all this stuff scattered about you. But go ahead."

"I'd rather wait, Senator, until it's completed.   In fact, I'd rather you'd wait and see it played," I replied, remembering what he had said about elevating the stage and fearing that he might object to some of my characters.

"All right.   But just now you said *our* play.   What do you mean by that?"

"I mean that a half interest belongs to you."

"Why, Lord bless you, my boy, I don't want to rob you."

"And I don't intend that you shall rob yourself.   You have given me the opportunity to do the work, you have —"

"Hold on, Belford.   We are partners in this house.   You are doing your share. Why, Sir, haven't you secured the Lamptons to play here a whole week during our county fair?   And doesn't that newspaper notice they sent along say that they are the finest representation of dramatic talent now on the road?   Haven't you signed a contract with Sanderson Hicks to give us the Lady of Lyons?   And I want to tell you that a man who saw such opportunities and seized them by the forelock is doing his duty all right. Oh, it's no laughing matter, Sir."

"That's all very well, Senator, but you are to own half the play. I want you to look after the business end of it."

"All right, Sir; all right. Yes, it would be better to have some man take hold of that part of it—some man, you understand, who isn't afraid to insist upon his rights. And Belford," he added, putting his hand on my shoulder, "if I hadn't insisted on mine, they would have trampled me under foot long ago. Yes, Sir (stepping back and shaking his hat), long ago. Have you decided as to who shall have it?"

"Well, it's easy enough for me to decide. But the decision of the other party might not be so easy to get."

"Oh, there won't be any trouble about that. No, Sir; that is, if they want to put on a good play. We have something here, Sir (slapping his hand upon the manuscript), that ought to stir the dramatic world from center to circumference. Oh, you may smile, but it will, for I want to tell you that I have never been associated with a failure. And there's a good deal in that; as sure as you live there is.   Luck begets luck, and failure suckles a failure.   Yes, Sir.   Have you made any overtures?"

"Not exactly.   I wrote to Copeland Moffet and send him a scenario—"

"A what?"

"An outline of the piece.   And he writes that he will be in Memphis on the 17th of next month, and that he would like to hear the play."

"Of course he would.   We knew that all the time.   We'll hop on a boat and go up there.   Good man, is he?"

"One of the best; he doesn't do things by halves."

"All right, Sir, he's our man, that is, if he's willing to pay for a good thing.   Well, I believe I'll go on out home.   It's cooler there.   By the way, come out with me. There's no one on the place except Sister Patsey, and I'm lonesome.   Come on, we'll ride out."

I was afraid to look at him; I was afraid

14

to hesitate, to frame an excuse, and without saying a word I went down stairs with him and got into the buggy.

He did not drive directly to his home; he halted at several places—in front of a lawyer's office, a butcher's shop, to ask advice concerning his political contest, a shrewd way to flatter and stimulate a lax supporter. We drove to a wagonmaker's shop, off in the edge of the town, and when the workman had been fed with big words, we set out at a brisk trot, with a gang of boys behind us, shouting in a cloud of dust. Ahead I could see nothing but the sun-dazzled roadway, sloping down into the open country, but we turned a corner thick with cherry trees and the Senator's house leaped into view.

It seemed a long time since I had heard the click of the gate-latch; since I had stood upon the stone steps to breathe the cool, sweet air of the hall.

"I think the library is about the coolest place in the house," said the Senator. "Step in, and I'll see if I can find some fans.

There are some on the table. Take that big palm leaf. Pardon me if I unbutton my collar. I'm as hot as a dog in August with a tin pan tied to his tail. But you appear to be cool enough."

"I didn't expect to hear you Southerners complain of the heat. I thought you could stand it."

"We do stand it, but we complain. I doubt whether an Anglo-Saxon can ever learn to like real hot weather. Oh, we prate about the sunny South and we like sunshine, but, by George, Sir, we hug the shade. Have you got a pretty good plot for your play?"

"Yes, I think so."

"We must have a good plot, you know; we must have everything turn out all right. Any fighting in it?"

"Well, there are several spirited scenes."

"That's good. But it strikes me that there ought to be some sort of a fight. One fellow ought to call another fellow a liar, or something of the sort. It would be a good thing for a fellow to snatch out his pistol and have it grabbed and turned against him, don't you see? That sort of a thing always catches the people."

" But you advocated the elevation of the stage, don't you remember?"

He got out of his chair, and walked up and down the room, with his collar unbuttoned, his broad, black cravat hanging loose.

" That's the point, Belford; that's the very point. To elevate the stage is to make it natural. Why, last season an actor ruined a play for this town by drawing a pistol with his left hand."

"But that was not so very unnatural," I replied. " He might have been left-handed. Many a left-handed man has had a fight."

He paused in his walk, to stand before me, and thoughtfully to balance himself alternately upon his heels and toes.

" But, Belford, that's not the point. Of course there may be a left-handed man in a fight, but nine chances to one a man is right-handed, and the stage must take the course that is the most probable. No, Sir, you don't want to shock a critical sense of fitness by having a man pull a pistol with his left hand. Such breaks always tend to wound a sensitive nature. Any man in your drama pull a pistol that way, Belford?"

"No, if a pistol is drawn at all it shall be in the accepted form."

"All right," he said, resuming his walk. "Any ragged girl talk like a clodhopper until she is insulted and then talk like a princess? Anybody say 'stronger?' No human being except a fool on the stage ever said 'stronger' for stranger. Any fat woman in short skirts trying to be a girl? Any tramp with more ability than an ancient philosopher? Any female detective that doesn't know she loves a suspected thief until she has had him put in jail? Got any of those things?"

"I'll take an oath that I have none of those tantalizing features, Senator."

"Then, Sir, it will be a go. Yes, Sir, the world can't stop it. Why, come in, Patsey. Remember Mr. Belford, don't you?"

I shook hands with the old lady, placed a chair for her and gave her my fan, and she rewarded me with an old-time courtesy.

"Gracious me," she said, "it's so hot down here that I wonder everybody doesn't take to the hills. I wouldn't live in this flat country."

"Why, Sister Patsey," the Senator spoke up, "Bolanyo is on a hill."

"A hill? Giles, you don't know what a real hill looks like, it's been so long since you saw one. Why, where I live you can sometimes look down on a cloud."

"Yes, and it's a good deal better to live above a cloud than to be under one, Sister Patsey."

"Now, what does he mean? One of his sly tricks, I'll be bound. I never come down here that everybody ain't up to tricks or running for office, but I do reckon they are one and the same thing. Sakes alive, and the laziest folks that ever moped on the face of the earth. And that good-for-nothing wretch that calls himself the Notorious Bugg, a-talking about his sons-in-law a-shaking all the time. He came here yesterday and wanted meat, the lazy whelp. Well, I would have given him scalding water, and a heap of it."

"But you didn't, Sister Patsey," the Senator spoke up. "You called him back and gave him a bag of sweet cakes."

"I did, eh? I sent them to the poor little children, and if he takes a bite of one of them cakes I hope it will choke him to death. He says he doesn't want to go to the hills and catch a new-fangled disease. Why, plague take his picture, I've lived in the hills all my life. If he comes again while I'm on the place I'll scald him. I'll do it, Giles, as sure as he comes, and you'd better tell him to stay away."

"If he comes again, Sister Patsey, you'll give him hot cakes instead of hot water."

"Did you hear that, Mr. Belford? *Did* you hear that?" the old lady snapped. "Ah, ah, I do think, Giles, you are the most aggravating man I ever saw, except your brother, and he almost worried the life out of me."

"But he is dead, Sister Patsey, and you are still enjoying pretty fair health.　Yes, he went first."

The Senator glanced at me with a wink; the old lady caught his twinkle of mischief, and, throwing back her head, she laughed until the tears ran out of her eyes.

"Belford," said the Senator, "the evening breeze has sprung up.　Suppose we sit out on the portico.　And, by the way, I've got some tobacco raised from Havana seed. I'll get it."

"Bring me a pipe, too, Giles," the old lady called after him.　"I'm not going to be left out, and you needn't think it, either."

When the Senator had strode off down the hall, she turned to me with a quick eagerness and said:　"He is almost dying to apologize to you for Tom Estell's behavior, and he doesn't know how to get at it.　I never saw a man so cut up.　And he thought he could get at it better out here, but by the way he fidgets about I know he hasn't. Now, there, don't you say a word, Sir, but let me talk. I don't know what's the matter with Estell, I really don't. Now, what earthly harm could there have been in her going fox-hunting, and her father along, too? No, I don't understand him. Why, he must think that a woman is a fool to be willing to stay at home all the time just because he's old."

"Why did she marry him?" I could not help but ask.

She snapped her eyes and cleared her throat. "Ah, Lord, it distressed me nearly to death. Why did she, indeed? Giles was the cause of it. He picked out a nice old gentleman for his daughter's husband— a man of high family, a good politician. She cried over it, with her head in my lap, but Giles didn't see a tear, and she wouldn't let me say a word to him. And, to tell the truth, I didn't think it was so very bad; and it *wasn't* until he got to be so cranky. She always was a peculiar child; and I reckon

after all she made up her mind that she
might as well marry one man as another, so
far as love was concerned.   But just look
at me, a-sitting up here and telling of things
that I oughtn't to say a word about.   Here
he comes. Giles, did you bring my pipe?
Well, it's a good thing you did, Sir."

Out in the breeze that came stirring
through the magnolia garden we sat and
smoked, the Senator with his chair tipped
back and his feet high up against a fluted
column.   We talked in pleasant and almost
confidential freedom, of many a home interest, both solemn and humorous, but the
name of the young woman lay under a silence
that no one dared to disturb.   When I arose
to take my leave they urged me to stay to
supper, but my heart had grown heavy with
the approach of night, and, with a lie in self-
defense, I pleaded an engagement in the
town.

CHAPTER XVII.

A SLOW STEP ON THE STAIRS.

IN the cool of the morning, and often at night when the gulf breeze was blowing, I leaned back from my labor to muse upon the Senator's peculiar attitude toward me. A certain sort of innocence or honor had unquestionably blunted his eyesight and wrapped his reason in a silken gauze, but he had seen and felt the interference of his daughter's husband. And now why should he have pressed me to come again to his house, even though the wife were away? The old woman had said that he was trying to find a way that might lead to an easy apology. Apology for what? A husband's clumsy resentment. And did he not know that my entering the house again could easily be construed as a connivance on his part? The politician is so absorbed a student of man and his masculine ways that sometimes he may be forgetful of the delicate film that surrounds a woman's name. But in the South a woman's name is so secure that what in colder regions might be a film is here a sheet of steel; and overconfidence might seem a want of due consideration.

One evening I heard a slow and heavy step on the stair; and I waited, annoyed and nervous with the deliberate and solemn approach of the unwelcome visitor. I counted the steps, wondering when they would cease. I threw down my pen and got out of my chair. There was a shuffling of awkward feet at the open door.

"Come in, Washington," I cried, and when he had entered I turned angrily upon him.

"Oh, you have come to reproach me, to prove to my face that I am a liar."

He had dropped his hat upon entering the

door, and now he stood with his head bowed meekly.

"Mr. Belford, if your heart smites you, don't blame me."

"But you have come to bid it smite me."

"No, but to ease it if it has been smiting you."

"Ah, sit down, Washington."

"I prefer to stand."

"But pick up your hat. Your humility embarrasses me."

"Let it lie there, Mr. Belford."

"Well, can't you do something? Damn it—"

"Mr. Belford, I don't ask you to respect me, but I command you to respect my holy calling."

"Rot! Well, go on; I do respect it. I beg your pardon. But why do you come here to hit me with the moral sandbag of a priest? Don't you know that any calling can be made offensive?"

"The gospel is always offensive to the sinner."

"Look here, you black impostor, I'll not put up with your insolence. Get out."

He stepped backward to the door, took up his hat, put it under his arm, and bowed to me.

"Wait a moment, Washington. Confound it, you always make me strut and talk like an actor. Let's get down off our high horses and turn them loose to graze. What did you come to say?"

"I came to beg you not to be worried because you were not able to keep your word with me."

"That's kind, but how do you know I was not able to keep it?"

"Old Miss Patsey told me that the Senator brought you home with him."

"And you know that *she* was not at home."

"Yes, I knew that she was over at the State capital, with her husband."

"They didn't tell me where she was."

"No, it was not necessary. They do

not blame you," he added, after a moment's pause.

"Then you are the only one who does blame me, except, perhaps, the Treasurer."

"Yes, the Treasurer who locked up the money of the State but forgot that a diamond was within reach of—"

"A thief," I suggested, and he bowed his head.

"Washington," said I, "you tell me that the Senator is blind and that the young woman herself does not suspect—" He shut me off with his uplifted hand.

"What I said then and what might exist now are two different things."

"Ah, then she does know now; she has gathered some of the wisdom that you have strewn about. You had seized the opportunity to be wise, and I had hoped that you would be harmless. But your wisdom is offensive. It seems that you would rejoice to have a hold on me."

"For what purpose, Mr. Belford?"

"Well, it isn't very clearly defined."

"No, Sir, and it never can be. Perhaps, after all, my discovery, if you please to call it such, wasn't due to wisdom but to an animal instinct. And even then it was a venture. You could have denied it better."

He came walking slowly forward, with his eyes fixed upon my writing-table.

"That is one thing I can't learn to do well," he said, gazing at my work. "My hand was too hard and stiff from labor before I went to school."

"Then you don't write your sermons?"

"No,. Sir, and Peter didn't write his."

"But you went to a college and Peter didn't."

"Ah, but Paul was learned of men, and Paul was the Master's greatest follower."

"Washington, you are surely a remarkable man. How old were you at the time you entered the university?"

"I don't know, Mr. Belford; I don't know how old I am now."

"Well, I have fought against you, but I

can't help believing that you are sincere. Here are five dollars for your church."

"Thankee, Sah; bleeged ter yer, Sah. I—I—I am profoundly grateful, Sir," he hastened to add, bowing in humiliation. "You must pardon the rude echo of my father's tongue.   Good-night."

CHAPTER XVIII.

TO MEET THE MANAGER.

THE Senator went with me to Memphis to meet Copeland Maffet. I was nervous and apprehensive of failure, but the old gentleman was steady and strong with the assurance of success. "You are worried," he said to me as we stood at the bow of the steamer. "Throw it off, for you are now associated with a man who has never been introduced to a failure. No, Sir, and they can't down us. When I first came out for office they told me that I had no earthly show. And what did I do? I took one fellow by the shoulders, turned him round and kicked him off the courthouse steps. One of my friends? Yes, he claimed he was, but let me tell you, Belford, that a man's gone if he lets his so-called friends run to him with discouragements. The only friend worthy of the name is the man who doesn't believe you can be beaten. I'd rather have a strong enemy than a weak friend."

We found Maffet waiting for us at a hotel. The Senator greeted him out of the gorgeousness of his effusive nature, and refused to be daunted by the cool, business air of the manager.

"Mr. Maffet," said the Statesman, "we have brought you something, Sir, that will astonish you. And, Sir, you'll not regret that you came all the way from New York to get a chance to put in your bid."

"I have other business that brought me here, Mr.—"

"That's all right, but you'll forget all about your other business before we are done with you. Ah, Belford, I've got a little knocking round to do, and I'll leave you to read your play to Mr. Maffet. Good old name. By the way, Mr. Maffet, are you related, Sir, to the Maffets of Virginia?"

"I think not.   My people settled in Vermont," said the manager.

"Same old family, Sir; best stock in England.   Won't you join us in a drink of some sort, Sir?"

"No, thank you, I've just got up from the table."

"Ah, yes, Sir.   But make yourself perfectly at home in this town.   I know a great many people here, and all my friends will be glad to welcome you.   And you'll find my friend here (motioning toward me) as bright as a judge and as straight as a string. Well, I'll be back by the time you get through with your reading."

I went with the manager to his room, and if he had been cool before, he now was freezing.

"Well, go ahead."

I read the first act, glancing at him from time to time; but no change passed over his implacable countenance.   He sat with his eyes shut.

"Go ahead."

I read the second act; but the droll representatives of a fun-growing soil did not crack the crust of his countenance.

"Well, go on."

I had now lost hope, and with scarcely a pause I hurried to the end of the last act. He opened his eyes, got up, walked to the window, looked out, whistled softly and then turned to me.

"You've got some great people there. The comedy part is excellent."

"Ah, you don't laugh at comedy," I was bold enough to declare.

"Well, not when I'm buying it. Let me have it a moment."

He stepped forward with a look of interest in his eyes, and took the play.

"In Magnolia Land, by—what's this? By The Elephant? What do you mean by that?"

"My pen name."

"Oh, it's all right enough; odd, and that counts."

"And if you decide to take the play, I

don't want my name known; and if any speculation should arise as to who the Elephant may be, you are to say you don't know, even if anyone should assert positively that I am the man. I want it to be a winner before I acknowledge it.''

''All right. It will raise newspaper talk, and that would help. Yes, I'll agree to put it on if we can come to terms, and especially if you'll consent to consider the suggestions which I may send to you. A play, you know, is never finished. I'll read it over carefully and make notes. As this is your first venture you can't very well expect an advance royalty.''

I had not expected it, and I did not ask it. Indeed, I was delighted with the prospect of a production, and I began to think that there must be something in my alliance with a man who never had made the acquaintance of a failure. We agreed upon a percentage of gross receipts, and went down stairs to dictate the contract to the hotel stenographer. And just as we were ready for his name the Senator walked in.

"We insist that it shall be put on in good shape," said he, assuming that the deal had of course been made. "Let me see the contract. Yes," he said, when he had looked at the top, the middle and the bottom, "that appears to be about the proper thing. Just let me put my name on it. But we must have witnesses, eh? Well, you just wait till I go out and bring in two of as fine gentlemen as you ever saw, from two of our oldest families, Sir. One of them can write as fine a hand as you can catch up with anywhere; he used to be Clerk of our House of Representatives. Wait till I go after them."

"Oh, anybody will do, Colonel," the manager replied. "I haven't time to wait on an old family."

"All right," said the Senator, with his hat in the air. "If you don't recognize the advantage of respectability, I shall not insist upon it. We'll get these two hotel

clerks back here.　They look like gentlemen, Sir."

Many a day had gone by since my longing
heart had fluttered with lightness.　And
now it was beating high with an exultant
hope; but its time of joy was short.　The
memory of a deep voice weighted it with
sadness—a voice and the words:　"Any
man can make a promise, but sometimes
it requires a *gentleman* to break one."

As we stood in the bow of the boat and
gazed toward the lights on the wharf at
Bolanyo, the Senator put his hand upon
my arm and said:　"My boy, that fellow
Maffet is a shrewd fellow, from shrewd
Yankee stock, and he would have cheated
you out of your teeth if I hadn't come along.
Yes, Sir, out of your teeth."

CHAPTER XIX.

BURN THE JUNIPER.

IN the enthusiasm of my dramatic occupation the figures forming in my mind had draped, as with a merciful curtain, the picture in my heart—had hidden the eyes. But now that the figures were sent away the curtain, too, was gone, and the image was bold with a new vividness. I resorted to numerous devices, walking, rowing, reading, but the picture was always before me, thrown from within; and at night, alone in my room, I could see in its vibrations the beating of my pulse.

The day of the scramble for office passed by, and the Senator and his son-in-law were elected; but Estell's majority was so small that his opponent declared that a fraud had been practiced, and gave warning that he would take his case to the courts. I met the Senator nearly every day, and sometimes we parted in embarrassment, when it would have seemed so natural for him to say "Come out to see me." But he did not say it; and out of his silence there came the information that his daughter was at home.

At last, in October, the theatrical season arrived, with a third-rate company to present "Virginius." I employed the columns of Petticord's newspaper, against the Senator's advice, had the town and a large part of the county well "papered," and when the opening night came round the house was crowded. I put young Elkin into the box office, and he must have been born for the place, for, although acquainted with almost every man, woman and child in the town, he recognized no one at the window.

Nervously I watched the people coming in, my gaze leaping from face to face. I turned away to attend to something, and when I came back and looked at the house

I knew that *she* was there, though I did not see her. The curtain went up and the play proceeded. On a sudden someone well in front cried out ''Burn the juniper!'' And then arose the yell, ''Throw him out!'' Several officers ran forward, and presently, in the midst of great confusion, they came back, almost dragging old Mason, the pilot, and Joe Vark, the shoemaker. Vark was the real offender, it appeared, and Mason was snatched up as an accessory. I went out with them, pleading with the officers not to use them roughly; and when we reached the pavement I demanded their release. The officers, glad enough to go back to the play, turned the culprits over to me. Both were drunk.

''Vark,'' said I, ''do you want to break up the performance?''

''Burn the juniper!'' he shouted.

''Now, here, Joe,'' the pilot pleaded, ''let's get something that we all understand —something like 'let her slide' or 'let her rip'—something we can all join in on.''

"I want them to burn the juniper. In the old days when the atmosphere in the theatre got foul they cried 'burn the juniper,' and I want it burned now. The air in there is foul with political rascality and scoundrelism. Burn the juniper!" he yelled at the top of his voice.

"Blame it all, Joe," Mason persisted, "let's get something that's down among the people."

"Gentlemen," said I, "you must keep quiet or I'll have you taken away. Vark, you don't want to injure me, do you?"

"No, I'm your friend, but you'll have to live here thirty years before I can declare my infatuation for you. Give a hundred dollars for a bonfire of juniper. And the long-lost sword of Mars was discovered by the bleeding hoof of a heifer, and was given to Attila. Burn the juniper!"

"Look here, boys, come back in and behave yourselves. Remember that the house is full of ladies, and that ought to make any man thoughtful in the South. Will you promise to behave if I let you go back?"

"I can't promise without juniper," the shoemaker declared. "The twelve vultures represented the twelve hundred years of the glory of Rome. Burn the juniper. Say, Belford, tell you what we'll do—we'll go down to Old Bradley's and take a drink as long as the horn of a wild steer. What do you say?"

"I can't go with you, Vark."

"Then I'll go back into the house and burn the juniper. No, I won't, Belford. You are a good fellow. There's nothing stuck up about you. And I'm sorry for that break I made in there. Shake. Now, come on, Mason, and we'll burn Old Bradley."

They went away, arm in arm, and out of a group of mottled idlers formed about the door came slouching the figure of the Notorious Bugg.

"Jest thought I'd stand here till the worst come to the worst, Mr. Belford," said he.

"I lowed to myself that if they jumped on you things would then happen fast and sudden. Hold on a minute and let me tell you. I reckon I'm as peaceable a man as you ever seen till I get too badly stirred, and then I can't compare myself to nothin' but a regular mowin' machine. Oh, I didn't want to come out till I had to. I wouldn't mind whalin' both of 'em, but the fact is, I wan't prepared to meet old Joe. I owe him for a pair of boots, and the most danger-some lookin' thing I ever seen is a feller that I owe. When I owe a man it appears like he can grow ten feet in a night, and sometimes when I step out into society I find myself in a wilderness of giants, I tell you. But I was jest about to thrash both them fellers when they went away, and in view of that fact I think you ought to let me go into your show."

I did not take issue with his appeal; I passed him in, amused at the thought that two of my characters had been thrown out of my house and that another one had entered, firm in the rascally belief that he had convinced me of his courage and his determination to risk his blood in the defense of my dignity.

The final curtain fell, and I stood near the door, not to receive congratulations upon the bad performance, but to seek food for my eyes. Miss Rodney stopped to tell me of her delightful evening. Bugg Peters hung back to say that the "hoarse feller with the table cloth wrapped round him wan't no slouch." I saw the Senator coming, gesticulating, talking. I saw *her*. I saw her face turn pale and then to pink as she approached. The Senator did not appear to see me, so busy was he with explaining to an acquaintance the merit of the performance; and he would have led her by, but in a burst of frank energy she broke loose from him and held out her hand to me.

"Why, Belford," said the Senator, "I didn't see you. Great show, Sir. Fine piece of work, eh, Florence?"

"I didn't think so, but I confess that I'm

not much of a judge," she answered, smiling at me.

"Oh, well, it has its faults, and so have we all, but it was an infamous shame that we couldn't open here without a disturbance."

"Yes," said I, "but those two men gave a better piece of acting than we could find on any stage."

"Oh, yes. Good fellows when sober, Sir. The pilot's family is all right. I don't know anything about Vark's people, but he'll do well enough when sober, Sir. Well, Florence."

He led her away, and she looked back with a nod and a smile—a bright and graceful picture as she passed through the outer door. And all that night I saw her, always led away, but always looking back with a nod and a smile.

CHAPTER XX.

GLEANING THE FIELD.

A VAGABOND artist came to town and
I employed him to make sketches
of Peters, Mason and Vark.   It was
easy to get a pose from the pilot
and the notorious one, but after his "juniper
spree" the shoemaker had locked himself in
his shop.   But we hammered his door day
after day, and one morning we heard the
sliding of the bolt.

"Come in," said Vark.   "But let me tell
you that I am in no shape to do work."

He had spread a blanket on the floor,
with a bundle of leather at one end, and
with books scattered about.   I took up two
volumes to find the plays of Marlowe and
the snarling complaint of old Hobbs.

"What do you want, boys?"

"I want you to stand for a few moments just as you are," said I.

"For a picture? What do you want with a picture of me? I'm nobody."

"Oh, yes. You've lived here thirty years, you know."

"All right, go ahead. I don't suppose there ever was a man so no-account that he didn't think his picture was worth something. But I wish you'd hurry up and get through with me. I wouldn't have let you in, but I didn't want to be rude to a stranger. Scratch fast, you chap!" he added, speaking to the artist. "What are you going to do with the sketch? Hang it up for a scarecrow? Done with me? Take it away. I don't want to see it."

He turned us out and bolted his door; and I heard him swear at his rusty joints as he got down upon the blanket and wallowed in the midst of his books.

I procured a number of photographs of gardens and of time-softened houses; I jotted down numerous hints of "atmosphere," wrote a full description of Washington and of Aunt Patsey and sent the whole to Maffet. And it seemed that these acts of gleaning were long to be protracted, for odd bits of characteristic color were constantly arising, as tinted mists from the soil. In nowise could they find a place in the action or the dialogue, but they would aid the stage craftsman to clothe his trickery in the garb of truth. But these color-mists came only of their own will, and never would they arise at command, to enshroud and to soften the vividness of the picture that tantalized me. Love may be a divine essence, calm as God-ordered peace, when it flows from the legitimate heart—it may be—but my love was *wolfish*.

The Senator was very much elated over the success of our Virginius engagement. Early one morning as I sat looking from the window, with my nostrils full of the dusty smell of sprinkled floors newly swept, he came whistling up the stairs.

"Ha! dreaming," he cried. "I can see it

in your face.   But you can afford to dream.
Keep your seat.   I don't care to sit down.
Well, Sir, old Zeb Harkrider hailed me this
morning to tell me that a good many of our
citizens didn't like our show.   I said: 'Look
here, Zeb, I thought I kicked you off the
courthouse steps for bringing me news that
I didn't want to hear a long time ago.
Don't you remember it?'   He remembered.
He didn't say so, but he stepped back.
'Why, I didn't know you were interested in
it,' said he.   I had to lie just a little, Belford.   I hold, Sir, that we are justified in
occasionally slipping a lie on our left arm
and using it for a shield, to protect our pri-
vate grounds against invasion.   Yes, I lied
to him a little; I told him that my only interest lay in the fact that it was my desire to
see our people well entertained, and that the
habit of constant grumbling would finally
blind us to the beauties of even the best of
things. So I got rid of him. And do you realize that Petticord didn't do us justice? Confound his insolence, you passed in his entire

brigade, and yet he says that only those who were easily pleased came near getting the worth of their money. That scoundrel suspects that I have a hand in this, and he would almost be willing to cut his own throat in order to do me a harmful turn. But I will get him one of these days—yes, Sir, I'll get him or drive him out of this community. My boy, you don't seem to be in very good spirits. What's the matter? Getting tired of Bolanyo?"

I answered with what the humorist of the "profession" would have phrased a "property laugh." "No, Senator, I am not getting tired. In fact, I would rather be here than in any place under the sun."

"Strong, but that's right. I was afraid that you felt yourself chained."

"You might fasten me here with links of rusty iron, but in my eyes they'd be a chain of gold."

"What's that?"

He startled me with the sharp eye of comprehension, and I felt myself droop under the look that he gave me. "I mean that this soft and restful air and the sweet breath of the gardens would exalt a soul in spite of the restraints of the body."

Innocence flew back to his eye. "That's good, Belford; I have felt it many a time. I have thought in moments of ambition that my talents as a Legislator were crippled here, that I might go to Congress, and perhaps make a National name for myself, but then came the idea that to broaden my scope might forever spoil my love for old Bolanyo."

He stood there meditating, with nothing more to say; he took out a small bunch of keys, looked at them and returned them to his pocket; he put his hands behind him; he went to the window and looked out upon the deliberate commerce of the town—wagons loaded with hay, carts of kindling wood, negroes with chickens, groups of story-telling countrymen.

"But I didn't know that the town could take quite so strong a hold on a stranger," he said, with his eyes in the street. "But, Belford," and now he turned to me, "you are a man of quick endearments, and so am I; and that is one of the reasons why I like you, and a reason, I might say, why I condemn myself. But I like a man or don't, almost at the start. They call me a shrewd politician, and I am, but I'm one of the easiest men taken in you ever saw. Oh, I can tell whether or not a man is a rascal, and I sometimes buy his ware knowing that I myself am sold, but I can't help it. One single note in a man's voice sometimes catches me—a little thing that he doesn't know himself. Belford, I want you to go to the State capital with me sometime, after the Legislature meets. I'll show you some of the most picturesque and genial old blatherskites you ever saw. Well, I've got some knocking around to do. See you again soon."

And it was thus that we always parted—with "See you again soon," and never with "You must come to see me." I wondered whether his daughter had warned him against the impropriety of inviting me to the house. I mused over the sharp light of comprehension in his eye, and made an additional trouble for myself with speculating upon the degree of his suspicion.

In the afternoon I walked far out beyond the limits of the town, not at first in the direction of the Senator's house, but I cut a quarter circle to the left and came upon the road that led past his gate. So self-forgetful had been my employment that I did not realize until I stepped into the shade of a cottonwood how hot it had been out on the blazing commons. On the dying grass I sat, with my feet in a gully, fanning with my hat, harvesting delicious shudders of coolness. From afar off came the hum of a thrashing machine, and almost in my ear an insect sang the melancholy tune that tells of autumn's coming. I heard the slow and heavy trot of an old horse, and around a bend in the road a buggy came, and in it a woman. I got up with my blood leaping. I stepped to the roadside and stood there, with my face turned away, and suddenly the horse fell back to a walk, in obedience to an impulsive pull upon the lines, my eager and outlawed heart had told me. I turned about. Her eyes were averted, and her face was red, and she would have passed without a word, without a look, but I stepped out boldly and cried: "Just a moment, please. The hame strap has come unbuckled."

"Oh, thank you," she said, and the horse stopped. I stepped in front and began to pull at the strap.

"Quite a surprise to see you, Mrs. Estell."

"Yes. But I don't know why it should be. I drive about a good deal."

"And I walk about a good deal, and yet this is the first time—"

"Can't you fasten it?"

"Yes; now it's all right." I stood partly in front of the horse, with my hand on the shaft. She gathered up the lines.

"Mrs. Estell, I hope you are not offended at me."

She laughed with music though not with mirth, and then her face grew serious as she said: "Of course not, Mr. Belford."

Where was the freedom, the outbreak of energy she had shown in the opera house; where was the look of frankness? All now was reserve, a cool and sacred respect for the law that held her tied with a frost-covered rope. I did not presume that she loved me, but I knew that she hated *him*.

"Have you buckled the strap?"

"Yes, madam."

"Thank you."

At that moment a buggy with two men in it came rattling by. One man turned to look back, and I recognized Petticord, the editor.

"Mrs. Estell, I hope sometime to tell you—"

"Don't tell me anything, Mr. Belford. Let me go, please. Good-bye."

CHAPTER XXI.

THE WORK OF A SCOUNDREL.

I WAS more than miserable all that night; I was wretched. I had betrayed myself, and now to show even the slightest interest in her was to imply an insult. But what could I hope for at best? My chain might be gold, but it was a chain after all, and must be broken. I would tell the Senator that I must go away; and the next day I sat, expecting his step on the stairs. And late in the day there came a step, but not his. It was not a step, but a bound and a rush. Young Elkin sprung into the room with a copy of Petticord's paper in his hand.

"Look what that scoundrel has done!" he cried.

I snatched the paper. One glance and

everything whirled round. I remember that Elkin caught hold of me; I can recall that I leaned against the casement of the window to hold the paper where the light was strong. I went out, down the back way, and through an alley into a silent street. I passed the lamp-post where the negro preacher and I had parted one night; I passed the goblin thicket. And now a cold dread fell upon me. What sort of light should now I find in the eyes of that old man? I shuddered at the thought of meeting him. I would rather have met a lion. His rage would drive me mad.

The door was opened by the negress. She nodded toward the library. All was still. I stepped lightly to the door. The Senator was moving about as if looking for something. I tapped on the door facing and he looked round.

"Ah, come in, Belford."

A tremor seized me. He had not seen the paper. "I was looking for an oil can," said he. "Put it down somewhere just a moment ago. Here it is. Looks as if we'd have a little rain."

He took up a pistol and began to oil the lock, moving the hammer up and down to assure himself that it worked easily. "I guess that's all right. Now what did I do with that other pistol?"

"In my room," a voice replied. I turned about with a start. Mrs. Estell stood in the door. She bowed. A cool smile parted her pale lips.

"Bring it, please," said the Senator.

She dropped a graceful courtesy, one that might have been seen in the gracious days of our grandmothers, and ran up the stairway. When she returned the Senator was standing near the door, but she passed him and handed the pistol to me. She gave me a look, and if now her eyes were glad, they were glad like a fire that rejoices to burn. Just one look and then she bowed and withdrew without a word.

"Let me oil it and by that time the buggy will be ready," said the Senator. "I think you will find it all right," he remarked, as he returned the pistol to me. The negress appeared at the door. "Buggy ready? All right. Come, Belford."

Not a word was spoken until we were far into the town, and then the Senator said: "If there's but one he belongs to me. Do you understand?"

"Yes, but he doesn't belong to you unless you can shoot first."

He looked at me, and beneath his gray mustache was a smile as sharp as a sword.

The horse was trotting at the top of his speed. We whirled round a corner, the wheels ground against the curb and we leaped out. A negro with his arms full of newspapers stood on the pavement.

"Throw them in the gutter!" the Senator commanded, and the negro obeyed. Up the stairway we rushed, into a corridor. The Senator tried a door. It would not open.

"He has locked himself in. Here, we'll break it down with this."

We gathered up a heavy bench, battered the door down and rushed into the room. The place was vacant.   We looked at each other.   A gust of wind stirred the papers lying about; a "bunch of copy" fluttered on the editor's desk.

"We'll find him."

We went into the business office.   No one was there.   We stepped out into the street, and there we were arrested on a peace warrant sworn out by Petticord.

"We must respect the law," the Senator remarked as we walked off with the constable.   "I mean the active presence of the law," he added, evidently recalling the fact that we had broken down a door. "We'll go over here and give bond, but we'll get him.   Yes, Sir, we'll get him as sure as you are born."

Bonds were prepared, accepted, and we were released.   The Justice followed us out. "Giles," said he, "I am awfully sorry that you didn't have a chance to kill him.   Never was a greater outrage perpetrated in this community."

"Yes, but I'll get him, Perry," the Senator replied.

"Get him? Of course! Mr. Belford, this makes you a permanent resident of our city, Sir. You can't afford to go away now, even if you have thought of such a thing. Giles, he swore out the warrant and got on a train at once, and I reckon his wife will run his paper. Is Estell at home?"

"No, he is over at Jackson. He'll be home to-night."

"Well, I'm sorry—but look here, Giles, after all it is simply an annoyance. That fellow Petticord has no weight."

"A man of no family whatever," said the Senator. "And, Sir, neither is a dog, but we may be forced to kill him. Come, Belford."

Together we walked back to the buggy. A street lamp, the first one lighted, flashed across the way, and I thought of the coming of Estell.

" Get in," said the old gentleman, "and I will drive you to—to your office." And as we drove along he added: "I don't know what to say. But don't think that I attach any blame to you. My daughter's word as to your conduct toward her, your consideration and your gentleness weigh like holy writ. And you know why I have not invited you to the house. But we'll say nothing about that."

" No, we can't talk of that, Senator. But there is something I must say. Let the horse walk, please. First let me tell you that I respect you more—love you more, if you will permit me to say it—than any man on the earth. I—"

" Don't, don't, Belford," he protested with a catch like a sob in his voice. "Don't."

And we drove in silence until we reached a corner near the opera house, and then I requested him to let me get out. He gave me his hand; I gripped it hard, and we parted without a word.

CHAPTER XXII.

IN THE THICKET.

ALONE in my room I sat, with the window shades pulled down, waiting for the coming of another day. And for what end? To meet the gaze of vulgar eyes. The tavern bells had rung the supper hour, and doors were closing about the public square. I heard the ''haw haw'' and the shuffling dance of negroes on the pavement. I heard Washington's step on the stair and I lighted the gas and waited, for now he was not an unwelcome visitor. He tapped at the door like a small bird pecking on a tree. I bade him come in, and as he entered he dropped his hat on the floor.

''Don't do that,'' I commanded, ''don't give me any more affectation. You despise your father's dialect but you preserve his tricks of slavish humility."

"Humility is more the virtue of the Christian than the trick of the slave, Mr. Belford," he replied. "But tell me why you are so free and simple when you talk to other people and so—pardon me if I use the word theatric—so theatric with me."

"Because you rob me of my naturalness and compel me to strut. But let me be natural now. Are you just from the house?"

"Yes, I came straight down here."

"Had the Senator returned?"

"Yes, but he soon went away again—after Mr. Estell came."

"Did you see them meet?"

"No, I had gone out to help the woman bring in the clothes because it looked like rain."

"And did the woman tell you anything about Mrs. Estell?"

"That she had locked herself in her room was all."

" And you didn't hear any talk between the Senator and Estell?"

" Only at the gate when the Senator drove off.   Then he said: 'Don't look for me until you see me.'   A boy went with him to bring the buggy back."

" Where could he have gone?"

" To take the train for New Orleans, to look for his man.   He had a telegram."

" And what did Estell say?"

" He swore as the Senator drove.   'By God,' he cried, 'you have gone after the wrong man.'   But perhaps I ought not to have told you this."

I strove to be calm, but almost in a rage I was now walking up and down the room.

"Yes, you should.   And the imbecile said that.   He ought to have his lying old tongue torn out."

" Be cautious, Mr. Belford.   The man—"

" The man what?" I demanded.

" May think he has a cause.   Wait a moment, please.   A cause to believe that you are in the young woman's heart, and

what more would he need to make him bitter toward you?   Be reasonable."

"You are right, Washington; you are
right.   But when we meet, what then?"

"You must not meet."

"But we might."

"You must go away."

"What, to blast her name?"

"No, to save a life.   Perhaps two lives."

"I will not go away.   There will be but
one life to forfeit—mine."

"Would that save her name, Mr. Belford?"

"Look here, you don't mean that the
people believe that newspaper's insinuation."

"They don't.   Representatives of the best
families have called to show their faith, but
what would they think if Estell should shoot
you?"

"And what would they think if I should
run away?   No, I will stay."

"Then I have nothing more to say, Mr.
Belford."

He strode out, catching up his hat at the door, and I counted the steps as he trod down the stairs.

Early the next morning I walked out from the town, but at no time did I turn toward the Senator's house. I went down the road that led through the cypress land, into the deep silence of the swamp. I passed the house of the Notorious Bugg, and I saw it trembling (a mere fancy, of course) with the shake of the aguish sons-in-law. A road, impassable except in the driest of seasons, wound about among deep pools of yellow slime. The ground shook under my careful tread, and the slightest jar was sufficient to disturb an acre of spongy desolation. I sat on a log with the feeling that no eye could see me. Sometimes the silence was so strained that it sang in my ear; sometimes I was startled by the flapping and the shriek of a gaunt bird, skimming the surface of the ooze. In this creepy solitude I took myself to task. Behind an error of the heart there stands a sophist, a

Libanius, to offer a specious consolation—
a voice ever ready to say, "It was not your
fault; you do not create your own desires
and neither can you control them." This is
true enough, but a man can control his ac-
tions. I should have gone away, for the com-
monest of sense had pointed out the weakness, the crime, of remaining. And what had
I hoped for? To tell her that I would wait,
with a hope ever warm in my heart. I could
not see a crime in that. But I could not
tell her—she would not permit me to lead
up to so embarrassing a subject. Washington was right. It was my duty to go
away, not to save myself, but to keep Estell's hands free of blood.

Strong in my resolve, I walked briskly
toward the town, and, coming out of the
swamp, I was still strong, but my heart fluttered when from a rise of ground I saw the
Senator's house, far away. To the left of the
road lay a piece of land, wild with briers and
a growth of new timber, a thicket check-
ered with cattle paths. Up the road I saw

a man coming, and, as he drew nearer, I recognized the slouching figure of Bugg Peters. I did not care to meet him, to be compelled to answer or evade his questions, so I turned aside into the thicket and brushed my way along a narrow path. On a sudden I leaped aside into a tangle of bushes. A pistol or gun had fired it seemed almost at my elbow. I listened, but heard not a sound. I thought I saw smoke arising off to my left, but it might have been mist, for the day was dark with vapors and low-hanging clouds. I was uneasy, and not knowing whither my path might lead, I turned back; and just as I reached the road a man and a boy, struggling through the undergrowth, ran past me. They said nothing, but, looking back with fright in their faces, ran off toward town. I looked about for Peters, but did not see him. I wondered what it all could mean.

Upon entering the town I avoided the busier streets, and passed through quiet byways. At the foot of the rear stairway leading to my room stood a man.

"Hold on," he said, and then shouted to someone above. A man came running down the steps.

"What's wanted?" I inquired.

"You," replied one of the men. "Come with us."

"But what do you want?"

"Come on quietly and you'll find out. Do you want us to handcuff you?"

I went with them, stupefied with astonishment. They would answer no questions. They took me to the jail, and then I was informed that I had been arrested on a warrant sworn out by J. W. Hilliard, charging me with the murder of Thomas Estell. In a daze I was pushed into a cell. I couldn't think; I had an impression that I had lost a part—the serious part—of my mind. I looked at the little things about me, a burnt match on the floor, a cobweb in an upper corner. I took up a tin candlestick and picked at a ridge of sperm; I sat down upon a cot, wondering if it would break under me, and I felt it shake and spring like the spongeland in the swamp. I heard the tavern bells ring, and I heard the tradesmen slamming their doors. And I even said to myself, "I shall be horror-stricken when I realize it all."

There came footsteps down the corridor, and I heard someone say, "All right, I won't stay long. Turn up your lamp. I can't see him."

The blaze of a lamp hanging in the corridor crept higher and I saw the shoemaker standing in front of my grated door.

"Mr. Belford, this is rough."

"Yes, it will be when I am able to believe it."

"I reckon it's so, and it won't take you long to believe it. But if you ever had cause to be cool, you've got that cause now. Brighten up. Several people have called to see you—the nigger preacher, too—but they couldn't get in."

"How did you get in?"

"The jailer owes me. Yes, and I worked my prerogative because I thought you'd like to see even a shoemaker."

"Tell me—tell me all about it."

"Why, Hilliard and his son was coming through the thicket. They heard a pistol close to them, they stumbled on Estell lying dead in the path, and they saw you making for the big road. And that slab-sided Peters says he saw you turn into the thicket. He heard the shot, and he ran in to see what was up, but couldn't find anything. It is a shame the way both those fellows were permitted to stand around and talk about it. It has made them mighty important. I dangled a debt over Bugg's head and silenced him, but I couldn't do anything with Hilliard. That scoundrel paid me about two months ago. Bad! It puts the Senator in an awkward position. He can't express an opinion, you know. Good thing he's away, gunning after Petticord. Oh, Bolanyo is coming up. They found Estell with his head almost blown off.

Seems as if somebody must have poked a pistol out of the bushes almost against the side of his head.   I am telling you all this so you may in a measure be prepared at the inquest to-morrow morning.   His watch and some small change was found, so it wasn't a murder for gain.   No pistol was found on him, so he wasn't expecting a fight."

"Look here, Vark, you don't believe I killed that man?"

"I haven't said so, but I'll tell you this —the people believe it.   You know it takes a great deal of argument to prove a stranger innocent and mighty little evidence to show him guilty.   In an old community it's a great crime to be a stranger.   Well, I must go.   The best thing you can do is to keep your head cool."

CHAPTER XXIII.

THE RINGING OF THE BELL.

I SAT down, in a full sense of it all, and reasoned upon the ugly happenings that stood to accuse me. Coincidents sometimes fit snugger than arrangements that have been carefully planned; they slip into place with a perverse trueness of adjustment. Thus I speculated, and I was astonished at my coolness. I turned about from my argument to notice that a heavy rain was falling. The courthouse bell was ringing furiously. The jailor came hastening down the corridor.

"What does that bell mean?" I inquired.

"God help you man, it means you!" he cried. "The signal for the mob."

"What! To hang me?"

"Yes, and I can't help you."

"But you can turn me out. Open this door!"

"I can't do that, Sir. They would hang me. They are coming."

There were no cries outside. There was the heavy tramping of feet and a tap on the door as if a quiet visitor sought admission.

"Who is that?" the jailor demanded, walking slowly down the corridor.

"Open the door, Hill."

"But who is it?"

"A party of friends. Open the door to your neighbors."

"But is it to the law—the sheriff?"

"The sheriff is locked up in the court-house. We want to be quiet about this thing, but —the sledge, Dave."

"Hold on, boys, don't break the door. What do you want?"

"A man."

And the man stood in the cell, placing a cool estimate upon each word and astonished at himself.

"Well, boys, I can't help myself, and when you take him you'll find him a piece of as dead grit as you ever run against."

I heard the bolt. He threw the door open. There was no rush, no noise, and not a word was spoken until the jailor opened the door of my cell, and then a man in a black mask quietly said: "We must trouble you to go along with us."

It was of no use to protest and I did not reply. With a small rope they tied my hands behind me and led me out into the street. And now there arose a yell. Rain was pouring down. The pine torches were extinguished. The lamps about the public square had been turned out. The mob was going to do its work by the light of a single lantern, borne by a man who strode beside me. In front of the courthouse stood a tree. Under it a large box was placed. A rope, with one end on the box, the other end lost in the darkness of the tree, looked in the rain like a waterspout. I heard someone say, " Keep quiet, everybody! " The lantern was placed on the box.

" Let me assist you to get up," said a polite man. I looked about, but saw no kindly face; I saw a circle of black masks. Suddenly the lantern was knocked off the box. A scramble followed in the dark and the rain. Someone seized my hands, something cold touched them, bore down hard and the rope fell apart. "Run through the courthouse," a whisper shot like a needle into my ear. I wheeled about; I knocked men down; and in the midst of a fury, an outcry, a stampede in hell, I stumbled up the courthouse steps, ran headlong through the black corridor, out the other side, into an alley. I scrambled over a fence, fell upon a shopkeeper's waste ground, stumbled over boxes, climbed over another fence—ran. Away from the square the gas-lamps were burning, and I shunned the light. The rain continued to pour, and the roadways were deserted. The speed of despair soon took me beyond the limits of the town, and now the darkness was intense. The sandiness of the soil gave warning that I was near the river, and I halted to listen, but the splash of the rain was all that I heard. Far behind me was a yellow smear—the town. But what was in front I knew not. I felt my way along. The ground sloped—the river. "If I could only find a boat," I mused. I walked up the shore, close to the water's edge, the ripples sucking the sand from under my feet. Once I fell with a splash, and I bore off to the right, to keep clear of the water, but a high bank had arisen between me and the outlying fields of darkness. Suddenly there came a loud splash. The sandy banks were caving in. I thought of turning back, and then came a splash behind me. I was caught in a trap of sand. There was nothing to do but to wait. I could not climb out, for I was now beneath a shelf, hollowed out under the bank, a crumbling roof. I sat down to wait for daylight. The river was rising. I was afraid to move. A yawn might have called down an ava-

18

lanche of sand. I could have plunged into the river, but I could not have swam against the current; I should have been swept down beyond Bolanyo, to be snatched up at daylight and hanged. And daylight was coming. The rain had ceased, but the air was heavy and I knew that the light would be slow. The yellow river grew distinct, close to the shore, and gradually, but with many a hang-back, it seemed, the light grew strong enough to reveal the walls and the roof of my prison. Overhead the sand was held by streaks of clay, but this support, I saw, must soon give in, for the current was eating fast. Up the stream, only a few feet away, was a whirlpool, where the bank had caved, and just below a strong suck was forming, but here was a slope, and I might climb out over it, though the way was treacherous. I did not hesitate, and struggling, clutching, on my knees, up again, the sand rolling under me, I fought and gained the firm ground above. Not a house was within sight. But I could see the plow on the dome in Bolanyo, miles away; and now it was a vulture, dark-limned against a darker sky. I trod across a gullied field, into the woods, to find a place to lie in hiding until night. I thought of blood-hounds. But the rain, the river and the caving sand were almost a sure protection against their merciless scent. Still I was frightened, and I walked for a long distance in a stream of water, with the old story of a runaway slave fresh in my mind. I could not even guess at the time of day. At the jail they had taken my watch, my penknife, money, everything. In a thick patch of briers I lay down beside a log and slept, and opening my eyes I saw a star. I bore off from the river, walking as fast as I could. I came upon a patch of yams, the southern-er's vaunted sweet potato, and fed raven-ously on the milky root. I passed numerous negro cabins and dogs barked at me. At daylight I hid again and slept.

In the evening of the fourth day I made bold to enter a negro's hut, always the refuge and the asylum of the outcast, and appealed to the generosity of an enormous fellow who reminded me of Washington. I told him I was a fugitive fleeing from the wrath of political enemies, and my story moved his simple and unsuspecting heart. He gave me food and a bed.

Thus I wandered night after night, heavy of heart, and yet with a prayer of gratitude. At last I reached the State of Illinois. One day in a cross-roads grocery where I had halted to split wood for a bit of cheese, I saw a handbill posted on the door. It set forth the enormity of my crime, attempted to describe me—tall, dark brown eyes, hair almost black, a straight nose and about thirty years of age; and they had paid me the compliment to add the word "graceful." They had added, also, that the sum of six thousand dollars would be paid for my capture. The groceryman and his friends were talking politics; and doubtless they had never given more than a moment's thought to a murder committed away down in Mississippi.

I believed that a city was my safest refuge, and I made straight for Chicago. There I might secure some sort of employment, and, under another name, earn money enough to take me to the wilds of the unknown West. I felt that a light would one day be thrown upon the mystery. But I knew that they would hang me, if they could, and then marvel at the light, should it ever come. I appreciated the fact that the hunt for me would not be given up. Six thousand dollars serve well to keep the blood of justice circulating.

I arrived in Chicago one evening, having spent more than two months on the devious path that led from Bolanyo; and the first attention to mark my arrival was the stare of a policeman. This threw me into a tremor and a cold sweat of fear; but he passed on without speaking to me, and I turned aside to walk slowly, and then almost to run in the opposite direction.

My appearance was against me. I was almost ragged, and I knew that it would be useless to apply for any except the meanest sort of employment. Times were hard, and even day labor was not easy to find. But at last, after a week of persistent application, of hunger, of shivering in the raw air, I was put to work in a livery-stable. They called me a "chambermaid," a "happy hit" in which they found no end of fun. Sometimes their jokes were rough, but I bore them with a pretense of good nature, passing on to my task; and one day my zeal found reward in the notice of the proprietor.

"Jarvis," said he, "you go about your work as if your mind is on it. Do you reckon you've got sense enough to drive a cab?"

"I think so, Sir."

"Well, have your stubble shaved off and I'll give you a trial."

"I'd rather not have the beard off, Sir. I have trouble with my throat."

"Well, we'll try you, anyway."

"In livery?" I could not help asking.

"What, ain't proud, are you?"

"Oh, no, but I'd rather not wear livery."

"It strikes me that anything would be an improvement over the clothes you've got on. But I guess we can fix you out. You must be from the country. An American farmer may wear patches, but he won't put on livery. We'll put you on a special, and you may start in to-morrow."

CHAPTER XXIV.

MAGNOLIA LAND.

MY wages were small, and I saved every possible penny; I gave up smoking, slept in the stable, and rarely paid more than fifteen cents for a meal. In my mind I settled upon the island of Vancouver, and I resolved to go as soon as I could save money enough to buy a suit of clothes and a railway ticket to Seattle. And from my exile I would dare write to the Senator. "Why not now?" I thought as I sat on my cab. "But he might believe the story set up by circumstances; he might long ago have condemned me as guilty of Estell's blood. And what must *she* think?" The beginning of my musings mattered not, for the end was always the same, with the woman. And in the night, when the fierce wind howled about the barn, with the stamping and snorting of horses beneath me, I lay in the dark and the cold, and gazed into my heart's illuminated memory. Her face was always frank and, though her lips were dumb, her eyes were full of whispers. "But what must she think now?" always came to drive her away into the dark and the cold.

In impatience, and sometimes in fear, I watched the slow growth of my savings. Once a man, a detective I was sure, came to the stable to ask, he said, concerning a woman whom I had that day driven to a railway station. He may have told the truth, but he put me in distress, and the next day when I counted my money I said, "I will go to-morrow." But on that day a paragraph leaped out of a newspaper and smote me. "In Magnolia Land" was soon to be produced at McVicker's Theatre. I had cause to believe that I was suspected of at least some sort of crookedness, since in my mind it was almost settled that the man had come to the stable to look me over in the hope of finding a "bargain," but I was resolved to take the risk to see the play. And I read the newspapers at night and at morning, nervous with the fear of finding an announcement that the drama was the work of a man now charged with the murder of Mississippi's Treasurer. As the time drew near the press agent multiplied his licks; the play was by a man who chose to call himself "The Elephant;" it had been read by "several of our leading dramatists and pronounced a masterpiece of originality, character, and strength." But to me the faith of Manager Maffet did not hold the piece above an ordinary experiment, a truth set forth by the meagerness of his "paper;" and, as nothing was said of the cast, I knew that my lines were not to be given over to well-known "people."

Would the day, which had sounded so near, never come! "Who are you?" a snail inquired of a wild pigeon. "I am

Time," the pigeon answered. "No," said the snail. "You may have been Time and you may be again, some day, but *I* am Time now."

In the evening I drove a drunken man to his home, four miles on the North Side, and when I helped him out in front of his door, he tried to hold me, to tell me that I was his friend, but I broke loose from him, and almost furiously I drove to the theatre. I had not time to go to the stable; I hired a boy to look after my horse, and hastened to buy a balcony ticket. The night was warm for the time of the year, but a threat of rain was in the air, and I was afraid that the house would be small, but the people kept sprinkling in, and I stood in a corner to watch them, uneasy and annoyed whenever anyone passed along, without even looking in toward the box office. The orchestra began with Dixie, and my blood tingled as I went up the stairs. Viewed from my seat, the lower part of the house appeared to be well filled and the balcony was crowded. I had not taken account of those who had gone in before I arrived. No program had been given to me and I was almost afraid to ask for one. I did not permit myself to speculate upon my misfortune, an outcast sneaking in to see his own play; I did not muse upon fate; I sat there with my pulse beating fast. But I did indulge the comfort of the thought that should the play prove a failure no one could discover the humiliation of the author.

The music ceased, the curtain went up, my heart leaped, and the soft beauty of the scene brought tears to my eyes. Could I believe it, there were Culpepper and Miss Hatch, their mouths full of "The Elephant's" words. A droll line, and the people laughed; a sentiment, and they applauded. So the ice was broken. The curtain went down with generous applause. Culpepper and Miss Hatch were called out; but I could hardly see them, for the foolish tears in my eyes. I knew that the acts to come were better and my heart swelled with the thought. There were many faults, of course, but good humor and enthusiasm do not hunt for flaws, and I laughed and cried and yearned to grasp the hand of a friend.

"What do you think of it?" I asked of a rough man who sat beside me.

"Great," he answered.

"Would you mind shaking hands with me?"

"I don't know you," he replied, "but I'm a good ways from home, and we'll call it a go. Put her there."

He thrust forth his hand. I grasped it and pressed it hard—the first I had touched in sentiment for many a day; and I was loth to let it go, but he was forbearing. "Shake again whenever you want to," he said. "A man that cries at a putty thing ain't a bad feller."

At the end of the third act there was a roar for the author, and at that moment I felt almost willing to risk my neck to thank those generous hearts.

It was over—and the great organ lifted its voice in triumph as the audience arose. But if I strode out with the tread of a conqueror, it was not unmixed with a sorrowful limp, the halting walk of one who sees the black word "bitterness" written upon the bright banner of his victory. A cold rain was falling. I stood against the wall to catch the echo of my achievement, the "good," "enjoyed it so much," "beautiful," of the hastening throng. The loud cab-calls ceased, and I stepped forward to drive my vehicle to the stable, when, glancing back, I saw something that almost wrung a cry from my heart. Beneath the awning stood the Senator and his daughter. I ran to my cab, threw money to the boy, seized the horse by the bridle, led him to the curb in front of the Senator, and bowing under the glistening drip I said, "Cab, Sir?"

"Yes," I think so," he replied. "We haven't far to go, just around yonder to the Great Northern Hotel. Let me help you in, Florence. I reckon they are right in saying that this place has about the worst climate in the world."

I held the door open until they were seated, and stood there in a tremble after I had closed it, yearning to make myself known to them. But the success of the play could not mean that I was innocent of an old man's death. They might never have believed me guilty. "I could throw myself upon their mercy," I mused. "But what if they should turn away with a cold word and a shudder?" Reason is the offspring of wisdom, but it has always been a coward.

"What are you waiting for?" the Senator inquired, with a tap on the window. "Drive on, please."

I mounted, not trusting myself to speak, and drove slowly away, with my eager ear bent low.

"Never saw anything like that play," said the Senator, "never did. But I tell you I was scared at first. Why, when that fellow Bugg Peters came out there I thought surely he would ruin the whole thing. And he was Bugg, up and up. Yes, thought he would spoil it all. Why, Florence, that fellow is the biggest liar on the earth!"

"But he is art, as we saw him to-night, Father."

"Well, yes. He said the very things that Bugg would have said. Yes, art all right enough, but whenever he *is*, art has turned out to be a monstrous liar. It does seem to me, however, that Bolanyo could have furnished a batch of more respectable characters—more representative, don't you understand—people of better standing. Washington is all right, an advancement, a high type of his race, but the pilot and the shoemaker are—oh, well, they don't represent us. And that old woman's meant for your Aunt Patsey as sure as you live. But in spite of these minor faults it is a beautiful play."

"I wonder," she said, after a moment of silence, "I wonder where Mr. Belford is to-night; if he could only have seen his victory; if—"

"Say, there, driver," the Senator cried, "why don't you go ahead? What do you want to halt along here for? I don't want to hurt your feelings, you understand, but I could have more than walked there by this time. Drive up, please."

We were now near the hotel. I drew up at the curb, jumped down and opened the cab door. The Senator got out. I did not look at him. I did not dare to feed my hungry eyes upon her face. He took her hand, and when she had stepped upon the pavement, she turned about. "Oh, wait a moment," she said, "my dress is caught. No, it isn't."

"I will settle with you in a moment," he remarked, looking back at me, as with haste, though with most gallant gentleness, he urged his daughter toward the door, out of the rain. I looked hard at her now, with my heart full of another night, when she had glanced back at me; I waited, gazing, en-

19

chained by her grace, until she reached the door, and then I sprung upon the cab and drove away. The Senator shouted, but I did not look around, until, turning a corner, I glanced back, to see him standing bareheaded in the rain, waving his hat at me.

CHAPTER XXV.

DOWN A DARK ALLEY.

SHE had wondered where I was, and the soft echo of her sympathy filled my heart with a psalm. Surely she could not have suspected me of Estell's blood. But the Senator — why did he break in as if impatient of my name? Had he grown weary with hearing it? But his interruption, it was not hard to believe, was more of a sorrow than an impatience.

I was near the stable now, but I stopped the horse, almost of a mind to turn back, to touch her hand, even if compelled to run away to hide again in fear and shame. I glanced down at my mean garb, I thought of the fierce aspect of my beard-gnarled face, and pride, not fear, forced me to hesitate. "But I will go early in the morning," I mused, as I drove on, still debating, the horse slow under the restraint of my sullenness. ''I will shave my face and—''

A man stepped out from the shadow into the light and raised his hand—the man who had put me in a tremor of fear. ''I want to see you a moment,'' he said.

I was near the sidewalk, at the mouth of an alley, and without a moment of speculation as to what the fellow might mean I leaped from the cab and darted into the alley. He raised a cry and I heard another noise, a pistol shot, perhaps. I plunged through an opening and scrambled over a great pile of scrap-iron; I tore open a frail gate and came out upon a street. People were passing, but they paid but little attention to me. I crossed the street, entered another alley, made as quick time as I could, and came out near the river.

All through the night I hastened onward, sometimes on a railway track and often in the mud of the prairie. My running away might have been foolish; the man might simply have wanted to make an inquiry. And, indeed, if he had settled upon me why had he waited so long? It was easy enough to reason, but reason when slower than action is a miserable cripple. I had money enough to pay my way out West, but caution dictated a fear of open travel, so I was resolved to walk in lonely places until I felt that to trust a railway train would be less of a risk. The rain increased with the coming of daylight, and I was driven to seek the shelter of a barn. A man came out to milk the cows.

"I have invited myself in out of the rain," said I, as he gave me a suspicious look.

"All right. A man ought to have sense enough to come in out of the rain. Which way are you traveling?"

"Looking for work," I answered.

"Well, you ought to be able to find it. But most men hunting for work these days put me in mind of a horse goin' along the road lookin' for somethin' to get scared at. A feller came along yesterday and said he was hungry; but when I showed him some work I wanted done he skulked off. Are you hungry enough to help build a fence?"

"No, but I'm hungry enough to pay for something to eat."

"Oh, well, then, I guess you're all right. Just go on to the house and make yourself to home."

I went to the house; and while sitting by the fire, the wind high and the rain lashing at the window, I formed the resolve to go back to Bolanyo. I would surrender myself to the authorities, to claim the right of trial by jury and to accept the result. And reason was not now a coward, a cripple, but more like a man, cool, bold and strong. I reviewed with pity the morbid fear that held me back from Maffet; I felt now that in safety I could have made myself known to him. The Senator had come to look after my interest, and surely he would not have frowned upon me. Yes, I would go back to Bolanyo. I was sick of the rabbitlike freedom of an outlaw.

"How far is it to the railway station?" I inquired of the farmer.

"Well," he drawled, "I don't know for certain."

I knew that it was not in his Yankee nature to give me a direct answer, so I waited.

"There's a milk station a little nearer than the other one. Want to get on the train?"

"Oh, no, I want to go over to the station to see how it looks in the rain."

"Which, the milk station or the other one? Ain't much to see over there, but the land's worth all of a hundred dollars an acre. But when we came out here from Connecticut it could have been bought for a song and they wouldn't have insisted on your carryin' the tune so mighty well. If you want to go jest to look, the milk station is as good as any and a good deal better than some; but if you want to get on the express train you'd better go to the other one."

"How far is it?"

"Which, the other one?"

"Yes, the other one.   How far is it?"

"Well, if you walk, it's—"

"I don't want to walk; I want you to drive me."

"Oh, well, if that's the case I guess we can fix it.   I'll drive you over for half a dollar.   The train will be along about dark or a little after.   You've got plenty of time."

"Have you a razor?"

"I guess I had the best razor you ever saw, but the woman (he meant his wife) took it one day and raked all the edge off it.   But I've got another one, a rattler."

"Would you mind my shaving with it?"

"Well, do you shave left-handed or right-handed?"

"Right-handed."

"That's what I was afraid of.   I shave left-handed, and if you change after the razor is set, why, it rather warps it, so to speak.   Neighbor of mine had a razor ruined that way.   It might not ruin mine, but I'm inclined to believe it would suffer about ten cents' worth."

"All right, I'll stand the damage. You grab after every penny in sight, I see."

"Well, I hadn't thought of that, but now that you put me in mind of it, I guess I will. And why not? Wheat down, can't give oats away, and hogs a-squealin' because they ain't worth nothin'. Everybody's got his teeth on edge agin the farmer, and if he don't grab at every penny in sight they'll have to lift him into a wagon and haul him to the poorhouse. I'll get the razor."

I heard him fussing about in an adjoining room, with a complaint, directed at his wife, that nothing could ever be found on the place, and presently he returned with the razor, a strop, a bar of soap and a dish of hot water. I looked at his bearded face and was tickled with conquest to notice his embarrassment. It was, however, but a brief season of defeat for him. His humorous shrewdness flew to his aid. "I guess," said he, "that my beard grows faster than anybody's you ever saw. I shaved not long ago, and shaved with my left hand, too— to keep my razor in the same shape and temper, you understand—but my beard grows so fast that I don't look like it. One of my neighbors tells me that I could make money growin' hair to stuff buggy cushions with, and maybe I could, but I never tried it; never had the time, somehow. Now, just hit her a lick or two on that strop and you'll be all right."

"You say your people came from Connecticut?"

"Yes, Sir, from right up the river."

"Did any of the family go on further South?"

"I think so. I had an uncle, younger a good deal than my daddy. He went South, married there and died in the war, on the rebel side. But he left Connecticut long before I was born. We tried to look up the family some time ago; I thought we'd like to have a warm place to go sometime in the winter; and, Sir, I got a letter from my cousin, tellin' me to come. He lives in Mississippi—name's Bugg Peters. Why, what are you so astonished at, Mister? It's a fact, and my name's Sam Peters. Well, I'll go out and hitch up the horse by the time you get shaved."

CHAPTER XXVI

CONCLUSION—IN THE GARDEN.

THROUGH the dark the train came with a stuttering roar. I turned to shake hands with Peters, but he had stepped from the platform to hold his horse.

"Good-bye," he shouted. "This horse has seen the train every day since he was born, but he'll run away if I don't hold him. But it runs in his family to be afraid of the railroad. His brother was killed by a train. Wish you well, and if you ever come this way again, stop off."

He was a skinflint and a rascal, but he had shortened a dreary day, and at parting I regretted that I had not told him of my acquaintance with his kinsman in the South.

With a change of cars, at daylight, I

could reach Memphis late in the afternoon, in time to continue my journey by boat to Bolanyo. I lay back, with my hat pulled down over my face, and strove to compose myself to sleep, and I dozed, but awoke at the solemn words of a judge, rumbling with the rythm of the train. Sometimes I argued that I was a fool to trust myself to the humor of an excitable people; but soon I discovered that this speculation was forced, that my mind refused to treat it seriously, that my hope stood, not at the bar, under the protection of the law, but in the Senator's garden. And from this height, in the redolent air, I could not force myself down to muse upon a long season in a cell, waiting for the court to convene.

Daylight came. I got off at a station, to step on board another train. I counted my money and found that I might have enough, upon reaching Memphis, to buy a suit of cheap clothes. But the most strenuous denial must be practiced; I could not afford food nor even a newspaper.

It was nearly four o'clock when the train arrived at Memphis. I hastened to the landing and learned that a boat would leave within half an hour and that fifty cents would secure a deck passage to Bolanyo. I was fitted out by a riverside clothier, and, after a quick "snack" of fish on a house-boat, I stepped on board the steamer that had brought the Senator and me with "Magnolia Land" up the river. I stood at the bow, and my heart leaped at the sight of the first green tinge in the woods. How soft and delicious was the atmosphere, after the raw wind of the prairies and the lake. How gently the sun went down, without a shiver, without a breath too cool.

I saw the lights of Bolanyo. And I felt about for something to touch—something to brace me against the surging of an overpowering emotion. I tried to picture the jail; I strove to recall the yell of the mob, the awful night, the tread of merciless feet; but I saw a blossom nodding in the sweet air; I heard a voice that filled my soul with trembling melody.

The boat touched the shore, and I leaped upon the landing, before the plank could be thrown out. And now a caution was necessary. To be recognized meant a night in jail, perhaps another mob, and it was my plan to go by lonely ways to the Senator's house and to surrender myself to him. In my haste I was almost breathless. I passed the lonely lamp-post and the thicket; I stood at the gate. I opened it without noise, and, with my heart bounding, I stole up the steps, raised the door-knocker and let it fall; and with the noise, the breaking of the metrical throb of the silence, I sprung aside, almost choking. Someone came slowly down the hall and fumbled at the lock. Would the door ever be opened? It was, and Washington stood before me.

"Ah!" he cried, seizing me in his arms.

"Come right in yere, Sah, Lawd bless yo' life. Let me hep you. Laws er massy,

de man kai hardly walk.   Yes, Sah, right
yere in de libery."

He lifted me in his mighty arms, carried
me into the library and eased me down upon
a chair.   "Now, Sah—Sir—let us try to be
cool; let us be strong with the love of the
Lord in our hearts."

He snatched up a hat and stood over me,
fanning my face.   "Yes, let us thank our
heavenly father."

"Where are they—she?" I asked.

"You must be cool, Mr. Belford.   Your
excitement might—might be bad for you all.
The Senator is out somewhere and so is
Miss Florence.   But you shall see them
soon.   Just quiet yourself down."

"I must see them—him at once, to surrender myself."

"Surrender yourself?   What for, Mr.
Belford?"

"Washington, don't force me to say it.
You know.   I have come back to give myself up, to stand my trial."

He ceased his fanning, stepped back and

looked at me. "Mr. Belford, haven't you seen the papers?"

"I have seen nothing. I have come to give myself up."

The hat fell from his hand. "Mr. Belford, you must prepare yourself to hear something. Let me be slow so that it may not excite you."

"Out with it. I can stand anything."

"Yes, Sir, but I must remember my failing, my father's rude tongue. But I will try to tell you in a civilized way. Once I told you of a woman I loved—now do not be impatient. You must wait, and if you are not cool you shall not see anyone. The husband of this woman was a sinner, and his wife kept urging him to join my church. One night not long ago, moved by the spirit, I talked to the hearts of men, and he was stricken with conviction. And the next day he came to me. He said that he was in the thicket and heard a pistol fire, and that not long afterward he came upon Estell's body with a pistol lying beside

20

it.   He looked about.   No one was in sight. He thrust his hand into the dead man's pocket and drew out a pocketbook and some papers.   Then he took up the pistol, but was afraid to touch the watch, knowing that it would be death to be found with it. Just then he thought he heard someone coming and he ran away, with the pocket-book, the papers and the pistol.   And one of the papers was a statement written by Estell.   He confessed that he had engaged in wild speculations, and that he was two hundred thousand dollars short in his account with the State.   He spoke of the commission which would be appointed to go through his books, and said that he could not face the disgrace—that death was his only recourse.   It has all come out in the newspapers, and the men who would have hanged you are willing now to make the most gracious amends.   They talk about you constantly, and they come every day to ask if we have had any news of you.   Why, yesterday a town meeting was held and our ablest speakers blew the horn of your praise."

"Where is *she?*" I demanded.

"She is out at present. Just be calm, and when the time comes you shall see her. The Senator went North to see the play. She went with him, and she hasn't been strong since; she was weak enough before. The Senator wrote to the man who has the play, some time ago, and told him that he would be held severely responsible for any mention of you in relation to the murder as it was then thought. And the editor? He sent a retraction to his paper; he acknowledged that he was a liar, and the Senator has let him come back to settle up his affairs."

"Did she—did she grieve?"

"Her life since then has been one of deepest grief, Mr. Belford, but not for *him.* And she sits in the garden every evening—waiting—and—and she is there now, Sir."

I leaped from the chair; I ran into the

garden, calling her name—not Mrs. Estell—
but "Florence! Florence!"

"Oh, who—who is calling me?" a voice
cried, and I saw her clinging to a tree for
support, near the bench where we had often
sat.   I ran to her, and the garden lamp light
was in her eyes as she looked at me.   I stood
in silence, looking at her.   I took her hand,
and in silence we sat down.   It was a long
time before we spoke.

"Oh, that awful night!" she said, with
her head bent low.   "There was no one to
help you, and when I heard the bell ring I
seized a knife from the kitchen and threw a
shawl over my head and ran down there to
stab the man that tied the rope.   I knocked
the lantern over and I cut the cords—"

Half blind, I saw my tears gleaming in
her hair.   "And when you stepped out of
the carriage the night of the play you
thought your dress was caught.   It was—I
caught it to kiss it."

"Oh!" she cried—and that was all. We
sat in silence, my tears gleaming in her hair.

And we heard a voice and a step and we stood up. The Senator came, with his hand thrust forth, feeling as if he were blind. And on my shoulder he put his arm, and it was heavy. And "My—my boy," was all he could say—"My boy."

THE END.

THIS BOOK HAS BEEN PRINTED
DURING MAY, 1897, BY THE
BLAKELY PRINTING COMPANY,
CHICAGO, FOR WAY & WILLIAMS.

www.ingramcontent.com/pod-product-compliance
Lightning Source LLC
Chambersburg PA
CBHW031030120726
47905CB00007B/2120